GRAND NATIONAL NIGHT

A Play in Three Acts

by

DOROTHY & CAMPBELL
CHRISTIE

I0154878

SAMUEL FRENCH LIMITED

LONDON

GRAND NATIONAL NIGHT

The play was performed for the first time at the New Theatre, Oxford, on Monday, November 19th, 1945, and subsequently at the Apollo Theatre, London, W.C.2, on Wednesday, June 12th, 1946, with the same cast of characters :

(In the order of their appearance.)

MORTON	*Charles Graves*
GERALD COATES	*Leslie Banks*
BABS COATES	*Hermione Baddeley*
PHILIP BALFOUR	*Frederick Lloyd*
JOYCE PENROSE	*Olga Edwardes*
BUNS DARLING	*Archibald Batty*
PINKIE COLLINS	*Hermione Baddeley*
DETECTIVE INSPECTOR AYLING ..	*Campbell Copelin*
SERGEANT GIBSON	*Vincent Holman*

The play produced by Claud Gurney.
The Set designed by Ruth Keating.

SYNOPSIS OF SCENES

The action of the play passes in the study of Gerald Coates' house in Chillington, near Liverpool.

PROLOGUE.—The night of Friday, March 27th.

ACT I—SCENE 1. The evening of Saturday, March 28th.

SCENE 2. The same evening (two and a half hours later.)

ACT II—The morning of Monday, April 6th.

ACT III—The same day (early afternoon).

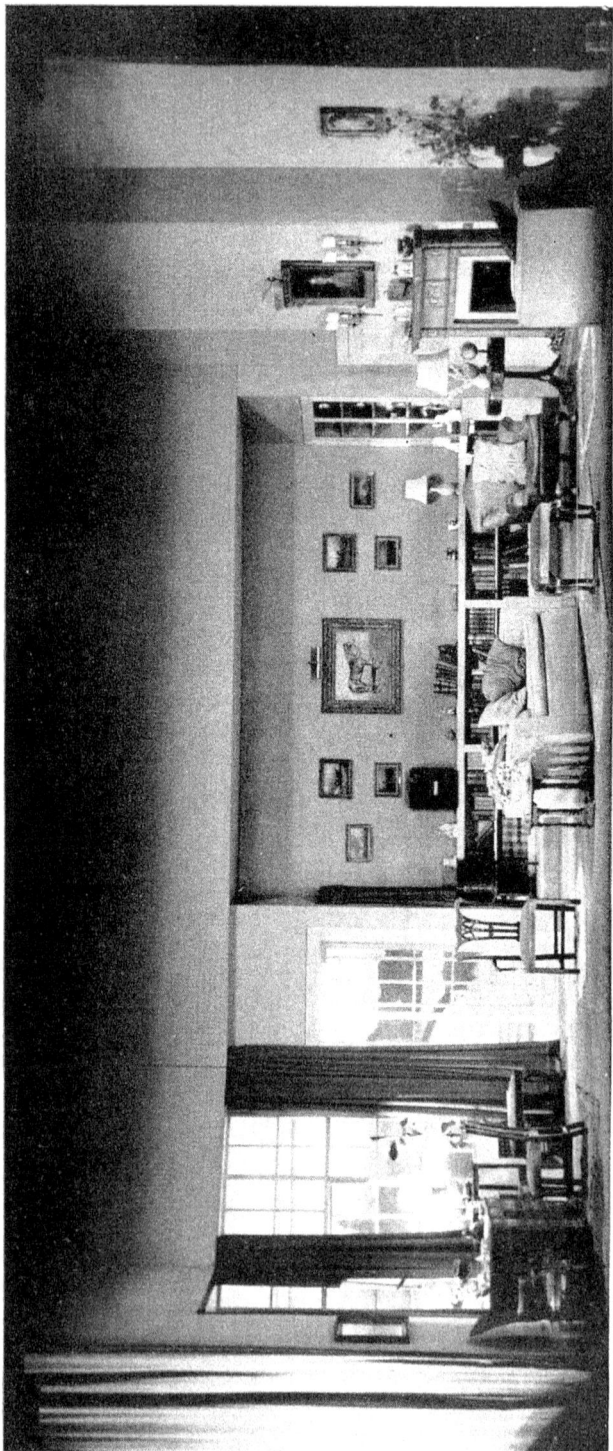

To face page 5—Grand National Night

GRAND NATIONAL NIGHT

PROLOGUE.

SCENE.—*The study in* GERALD COATES' *house, in Chillington, Lancs. Chillington is a village about twelve miles south-east of Liverpool. The time is about* 11 *p.m. on the night of March 27th.*

The room is large and pleasant and informal. The ceiling is low, and the furniture has been chosen and arranged with taste. The R. *wall is almost entirely taken up with windows which look out over the garden. They are closed and curtained now. The fireplace is in the centre of the* L. *wall ; a door up* L. *opens into the hall. Below the windows is a desk. The telephone stands on this. From the garden door up* R. *to the* L. *hand side of the room is an alcove which is lined with books at the back to a height of three feet. On the ledge formed by the top of the bookcase stand the odds and ends of ornaments and a small radio set. An oil painting of a Grand National winner hangs central in the alcove and each side of the picture are small sporting prints. At the* R. *of the alcove a small window overlooking the garden and at the* L. *a glass-fronted cupboard containing an imposing collection of silver racing cups. Over the fireplace hangs a life-size portrait of a very pretty girl in a dress about ten years out of date. There is no other picture near it, and it catches the eye at once.*

The lights are on, and a log fire is burning. A small table up-stage in the alcove holds a tray of drinks.

When the CURTAIN *rises* GERALD COATES, *who is in his late thirties, is lying on the settee, his head downstage, reading a book. He is wearing an old smoking jacket over his dinner clothes and is obviously settling down to a quiet evening's reading.* MORTON, *the old family retainer, is standing by the desk tidying up the local evening paper. He is old and very slow and deliberate in all his thoughts and movements. He puts the folded newspaper on the desk and slowly crosses to the door up* L. *The radio is softly playing a Gilbert and Sullivan selection.*

MORTON (*crossing up* L). Will that be all, sir ?

GERALD. Yes, thank you, Morton. You can go to bed now. I'll turn out the lights and lock up.

MORTON. Good night, sir.

GERALD. Good night, Morton.

(MORTON *reaches the door up* L. *and goes out.* GERALD *discovers a page in his book which has not been cut. He rises from the settee*

5

and crosses to the desk to fetch a heavy dagger-type paper knife. He takes this to the settee, settles down again, cuts the page and puts the knife down on the table at the back of the settee. Suddenly a sound is heard—someone tapping at a window. It comes from the garden door, which is hidden behind the drawn curtains. GERALD *does not hear it at first, but when the tapping is repeated, more loudly, he looks up sharply. He gets up and crosses the room, draws the end curtain from* L. *to* R. *and unbolts and opens the door.*)

GERALD (*standing* R. *of the door*). Hullo, Babs !

(BABS COATES *hovers on the threshold for an instant, then comes in, and passes him without a word. She crosses upstage and comes down* L. *of the settee to the fire. She drops her bag on the settee as she passes.* GERALD *shuts the door and draws the curtains again. Then he goes to the radio and turns if off.* BABS *is about thirty, and already running to fat. Drink has coarsened and spoilt what must once have been a lovely face. She is heavily made up and flashily dressed in a leopard-skin coat over a suit of red-and-brown check. She wears a scarf over her head and carries a big brown handbag.*)

I didn't expect you.

BABS. I got fed up and came back. (*She leans on the mantelpiece and warms her feet.*)

GERALD (*moving down to the* L. *end of the settee*). I'm sorry. (*He puts his book on the table above the settee.*) What went wrong ? I hoped you were enjoying yourself. Was it a good race ?

(BABS *shrugs her shoulders but does not answer.*)

Did you make any money ?

BABS. A bit. (*She moves down to the bell below the fireplace and rings it.*)

GERALD. What do you want ?

BABS. A drink. A glass.

GERALD (*moving to the door up* L.). Oh, I'll get you one. Morton's gone to bed.

BABS. God ! At eleven o'clock. Give me yours.

(GERALD *hesitates.*)

Other people's servants stay up till *they've* gone to bed. No, give me yours. I can't wait while you do the butler's work.

(GERALD *takes his glass from the table behind the settee and goes to the drinks table. He fills the glass.*)

(*Moving up* L. *of the settee to* GERALD.) Morton's a damn sight too old for his job. You ought to sack him.

(GERALD *hands her the glass.*)

Is there any whisky in that ?

GERALD. About half and half.
BABS (*without tasting it*). Morton's been watering it.

(BABS *holds out her glass, and* GERALD *adds more whisky.* BABS *tilts the decanter sharply, and then drinks.*)

That's better. (*She comes down to the fireplace.*)
GERALD. It's been a filthy day.
BABS. Yes, the wettest National for thirty-seven years.
GERALD. Did you have a bad drive down ?
BABS. Foul.
GERALD (*trying to hide his suspicion*). Who drove you down ?
BABS (*warming her feet at the fire*). Donovan.
GERALD (*disbelieving*). What have you done with him ?
BABS. I've sent him home. I'd had enough of him.
GERALD (*coming down to* L. *of the settee*). How's he getting home ?
BABS. He's walking.
GERALD (*still suspicious*). Why didn't you let him take the car ?
BABS. Because I want it in the morning. (*She turns to* GERALD *and snaps at him.*) Oh, he's all right—do let me manage my own business ! (*She sits in the arm-chair above the fire.*)

(GERALD *looks at her for an instant. He picks up his book from the table behind the settee.*)

GERALD (*coming to the front of the settee*). How was Pinkie ? (*He sits on the settee* C. *and reads.*)
BABS. Pinkie's all right. She's coming down to-morrow, staying till Wednesday.
GERALD (*reading*). Good !
BABS. And I've asked Buns Darling to dinner to-morrow.
GERALD (*reading*). Not so good.
BABS. I suppose I can ask who I like to dinner, can't I ?
GERALD. Yes, of course you can. (*He looks up from the book.*) Only I've asked Philip Balfour, I'm just wondering if they'll mix.
BABS. There's nothing wrong with Buns, is there ?—except that he's a friend of mine, of course.
GERALD (*ignoring this*). What have you done with your suitcase ?
BABS. It's in the car.
GERALD (*rising and moving towards the door up* L). I'll get it for you.
BABS (*jerking her head towards the window*). No, the car's that way. It's outside the garage.

(GERALD *crosses towards the garden door and stops up* R.C.)

GERALD (*turning*). Babs, *did* Donovan drive you down ?
BABS. I've said so once.
GERALD. I know, I'm asking you again. He wouldn't have left the car outside the garage, and he's not likely to walk home at this hour.

BABS. Well, if you want to know, I drove myself.

GERALD (*moving to the* L. *end of the settee*). Babs !

BABS (*rising and going to the fire*). God ! I knew there'd be a scene.

GERALD. Look here, Babs, I don't interfere with you much. As far as I'm concerned, you can go where you like, and do what you like, but I will not have you driving a car. Especially after dinner.

BABS. What's after dinner got to do with it ? (*She crosses below the settee to* R.C.) I've hardly had a drink all day. (*She goes to the drinks table and refills her glass. Truculently.*) Oh, go on—go on— say it ! You'd nag anyone into drinking.

GERALD (*moving to the arm-chair above the fire*). You know I'm past caring how much you drink.

BABS (*suddenly beginning to cry*). That's why I do ! You don't care for me any more ! You don't care what I do !

GERALD. It isn't worth your while to cry, and I won't be side-tracked. After the Skinner case you swore to me——

BABS (*coming to* R. *of the table behind the settee*). God ! I knew we'd get to Skinner in the end. Oh, all right, I know I killed him, but for God's sake let him lie. Anyway, it wasn't my fault. Skinner was drunk.

GERALD. It wasn't Skinner who was drunk.

BABS. Anyone'd think you'd suffered over Skinner ! *You* weren't stuck up in that filthy court ! You weren't booed by a crowd of dirty yokels ! (*She comes down to the small table* R. *of the settee.*)

GERALD. Now listen, Babs. Your licence was taken away for ten years. While you're living here, I'm responsible for you. The next time I find you've been driving a car, you'll leave this house and you'll never come back. You're seldom in a fit state to drive a car nowadays, and I won't have innocent people killed. (*He moves to the fire and leans on the mantelpiece.*)

BABS. Gerry ! (*She puts her glass on the table* R. *of the settee.*) Oh, God, I'm so miserable ! Gerry, don't talk to me like that ! (*She moves below the settee to the* L. *end.*)

GERALD. I blame Pinkie, too. She ought to have stopped you.

BABS. Pinkie didn't know—nobody knew. I didn't go back to Pinkie's after the racing, I dined at the Adelphi. (*She sits on the settee,* L. *end.*)

GERALD. Donovan, then—why didn't he stop you ?

BABS. He didn't know, either—I've told you, no one knew. Gerry, don't be horrid, don't be suspicious of me. Why should I lie to you ?

GERALD. You generally do. Now, please don't misunderstand me—I don't care a damn what you've been doing. I'm only interested in one thing—I want to know who let you drive yourself back.

BABS. I swear no one knew. And I was perfectly all right, I'd hardly drunk anything. (*She rises and takes off her coat.*) After dinner, I suddenly felt I must get back to you—I was sick of all that crowd. (*She throws her coat over the* L. *end of the settee.*) I didn't tell anyone I was coming, I just came. (*She goes towards* GERALD.)

GERALD. That might be the truth for once. (*He avoids her.*)

(BABS *begins to cry again.*)

I'll get your suit-case.

(GERALD *crosses downstage to the desk. He takes a torch out of the top* R. *drawer and switches it on. Then he goes out through the garden door.* BABS *moves to the settee and sits. She bends down to remove her shoes.*)

BABS (*taking off one shoe*). O-oh ! (*She draws in her breath painfully.*) Oo-oo ! (*The other shoe comes off.*) Oh, God ! (*She drops the shoes in front of the upstage end of the settee. For a moment or two she flexes her toes and rubs her feet.*)

(*The telephone rings.* BABS *looks at it and decides to let it ring unanswered. She beds down the cushion on the downstage arm of the settee and settles her head on it. She becomes annoyed with the telephone and rises. Without putting her shoes on she crosses downstage to the desk. She lifts the receiver.*)

Hullo ? (*She waits.*) Hullo ? (*She waits again, and then, very annoyed, shouts :*) WHO'S there ? Who's that ? (*She bangs down the receiver. She crosses to the table* R. *of the settee, takes her glass and goes up to the drinks table. She pours a drink and adds soda-water.*)

(MORTON *enters up* L.)

MORTON (*up* L.C.). You called, Madam ?

(*Startled,* BABS *spills her soda-water. She rounds on* MORTON *angrily.*)

BABS. You damn fool ! (*She bangs the syphon down on the table.*)
MORTON. You called ?
BABS. No, I didn't—I rang. I rang half an hour ago.
MORTON. I'm sorry, Madam, I was up in my room.
BABS. Well, didn't you hear the bell ?
MORTON. No, madam, I came downstairs to get something, and I heard your voice.
BABS (*moving down* L.C. *towards the fire*). You ought to have *been* downstairs—you ought to have heard the bell. I don't know why Mr. Coates keeps you, he won't keep you much longer—not if I can help it. You're too old, Morton, you're much too old for your

job—too old for any job. (*She turns at the fire.*) *And* you've been watering the whisky.

MORTON (*moving down a step between the settee and the arm-chair above the fire ; hurt and indignant*). No, madam.

BABS (*quite drunk now*). Yes, you have. That's what Colonel Daubeney sacked you for, wasn't it ? Wasn't it ? Or was it stealing the port ?

MORTON (*ignoring this*). Can I get you anything, Madam ?

BABS. No, you're far too late as usual, you can go back to bed.

MORTON. Good night, madam. (*He turns to go.*)

(BABS *goes to the settee and picks up her bag.*)

BABS. Here, you !

(MORTON *turns and comes to the end* L. *of the settee.*)

I've lost the mirror out of this bag. Have you seen it ? (*She sits on the settee.*)

MORTON. No, madam.

BABS. I had it here two days ago. If anyone ever cleaned this room, they'd have found it.

MORTON. I'll speak to Hoskyns in the morning.

BABS. No, you won't. I'll speak to her myself. That's another servant who ought to get the sack.

(MORTON *turns to go.*)

Oh, wait a minute. (*She picks up her shoes and throws them towards the fire.*) Get rid of these—they give me hell.

(MORTON *moves down to the fire and picks up the shoes.*)

That's all. Go on, get out.

MORTON (*going to the door up* L.). Good night, madam.

(*Exit* MORTON. BABS *takes a lipstick from her bag and makes up her mouth. After a moment* GERALD *enters by the garden door. He is carrying a suit case which he puts on the stool up* R. *He closes the door and draws the curtain ; then he comes down to the desk and replaces the torch in the drawer. He crosses below the settee to the fire.*)

BABS. Gerry, I'm so miserable. Oh Gerry, I'm sorry I drove myself back, I'm sorry ! I only did it because I couldn't bear to be away from you any longer. Aren't you a teeny weeny bit pleased to see me ? Gerry, you aren't jealous about Donovan, are you, darling ? I mean, you don't think there's anything between us—I mean, you know there's nothing. I swear I've never looked at another man since I married you. Oh, Gerry, can't we start again ? I'll give up drink, I swear I will ! I'll never touch another drop—never !

GERALD. Babs, I'm tired, and it's late, and you've been saying that for the last ten years.

BABS. I really mean it this time. Gerry, I mean it.

GERALD. And you always say that, too. I suggest you go to bed.

BABS (*rising*). I mean it this time, darling—I mean it . . . (*She goes to* GERALD *and tries to put her arms round his neck.*)

GERALD (*gently removing her arms*). You'd better go to bed. (*He crosses downstage to the desk.*)

BABS (*aware of his distaste*). Damn you ! Damn you ! So I'm not allowed to touch you. Now that I'm old, you don't care. (*She goes up* L. *of the settee.*) To think I could have married anyone ! *Anyone* I could have . . .

GERALD (*sitting at the desk*). Babs—please ! (*He puts his* R. *elbow on the desk and rests his head in his hand, wearily.*)

BABS. Babs—please ! I know what's the matter with you ! You've got someone else in line ! Who is she ? Come on, who is she ? You won't tell me, but I'll find out ! (*She comes down* L. *of the settee to the front and kneels on it. She faces* GERALD *across the* R. *arm.*) And when I find out the dirty bitch who's running after my husband, d'you know what I'll do ? (*She leans across the back of the settee ; her* R. *hand rests for a moment on the knife on the table behind. She is suddenly aware of it and grasps it.*) I'll show you what I'll do to her ! And by God, I'll start on you ! (*She gets down off the settee and crosses quickly to* GERALD.)

(GERALD *rises.* BABS *flings herself on him, knife in hand. The lights go out.*)

GERALD. Put down that knife !

CURTAIN.

ACT I.

Scene 1.

Scene. *The same. The evening of Saturday, March 28th.*

The curtains are closed and all the lights are on. Standing by the fire warming his hands is PHILIP BALFOUR, *an old solicitor friend of* GERALD'S. *He has a small goatee beard.*

Immediately the CURTAIN *rises,* GERALD *enters up* L. *He is dressed in a dinner jacket.*

GERALD. Hullo, Philip! Morton told me you were here. Sorry I have kept you waiting.

PHILIP. I was quite happy—just getting thawed out!

GERALD (*crossing to the drinks table*). Whisky?

PHILIP. Thanks. (*He turns to the fire.*) This is a nice fire.

GERALD. What's it like out? Still raining?

PHILIP. Pouring torrents. An abominable night.

GERALD. Say when.

PHILIP (*looking at the fire ; very promptly*). When.

GERALD (*coming down* L. *of the settee to* PHILIP). Sorry—have I drowned it? (*He gives* PHILIP *the glass.*)

PHILIP. Mm . . . it'll do.

GERALD. Were you at the National yesterday? (*He crosses downstage and goes up* C. *to the drinks table.*)

PHILIP. No, a series of importunate clients kept me in my office. (*He sits in the armchair above the fire.*)

GERALD (*pouring himself a whisky*). You ought to close down during the Aintree meeting.

PHILIP. A reputable solicitor could hardly do that, whatever you may do in the shipping world! I suppose you were there?

GERALD. No, worse luck! I was helping to bury Mrs. Carter.

PHILIP. True—I forgot. That must be the first National old Carter's ever missed.

(GERALD *comes down to the table behind the settee and puts his glass on it.*)

GERALD (*picking up the cigarette box*). It's the first I've missed for ten years. (*He offers the cigarettes to* PHILIP.)

PHILIP (*taking a cigarette*). Yes, your sense of responsibility is growing—slowly, and not before it was time. A few years ago you'd have had a sudden severe indisposition and dodged the cemetery.

GERALD. A few years ago I was riding in the damn race, and nothing would have kept me away. (*He takes a cigarette.*)

PHILIP. It's an unjust world.

12

GERALD. Possibly, but what brings it home to you suddenly ?

PHILIP. The virtuous clerks who stuck to their stools and made out bills of lading are still on their stools. It's the one who played truant to ride in every race meeting up and down the country who got the partnership. (*He lights his cigarette.*)

GERALD. Well, old Carter likes to see his horses win. (*He replaces the cigarette box on the table behind the settee.*)

PHILIP. I know he does. If you hadn't steered Dutch Prince round Aintree for him you wouldn't be where you are.

GERALD. The old Prince steered himself. (*He holds a light to his cigarette.*)

PHILIP. Well, you hadn't much to risk but your neck in those days. Where's Babs ? Not back from Aintree ?

(GERALD *pauses.*)

GERALD. No, I wasn't expecting her. She's staying with Pinkie. Oh, that reminds me, Philip—I've just had Mrs. Skinner here. (*He picks up his glass.*)

PHILIP. Aye, we met in the hall. What did she want ?

GERALD. She was rather worried, poor little thing.

PHILIP. I'm worried, too. I'm worried about that cheque you sent her. I shall have hard words from the Insurance Company, when they hear about it.

GERALD (*sitting on the arm of the settee*). That's your funeral. She can't starve while the insurance people haggle. Oh, I tore up that lovely piece of legal nonsense you gave her.

PHILIP. Oh ? What piece of nonsense was that ?

GERALD. Admitting she had no legal claim on me.

PHILIP (*taking out a note book*). Well, that'll cost you just seven-and-six to get it copied. I'll have that seen to first thing on Monday.

GERALD. Now listen, Philip, I hate this business—get it settled for me. I don't care what it costs. I can afford it.

PHILIP. I know you can, and we will settle it. I'm only taking reasonable legal precautions.

GERALD. The thing she seems to mind most is that between us we made it look as if it was Skinner who was drunk.

PHILIP. It was the only line of defence.

GERALD. A pretty rotten one. (*He finishes his drink.*)

PHILIP. I agree, but it got Babs off with a fine and the loss of her licence. It wouldn't have helped Mrs. Skinner to let Babs go to prison. It wouldn't have helped anyone.

GERALD (*moving to the fire*). No—quite. Oh well, for God's sake let's not talk about it. (*He puts his glass on the mantelpiece.*) There's only one thing that matters—I want Mrs. Skinner to be looked after.

PHILIP. I'll look after her. (*He hesitates.*) There's one other thing, and it arises more or less out of the Skinner case.

GERALD. Well ?

PHILIP. I don't think you'll much like my bringing it up . . .

GERALD (*bending down to put a log on the fire*). There's nothing about the Skinner case that I do like—much.

PHILIP. . . . and I wouldn't if I didn't have to. It's about Babs.

(GERALD *starts*.)

GERALD (*with a change of manner*). Oh ? (*He straightens up.*)

PHILIP. I knew you'd bristle. Remember, I said I had to.

GERALD (*dangerously*). Why ?

PHILIP. Because old Carter's been speaking to me.

GERALD (*crossing below the settee to* C.). Well, I wish to God Carter'd mind his own damned business.

(PHILIP *puts his glass on the table above the fire.*)

PHILIP (*rising ; patiently*). He thinks it is his business. (*He moves down to the fire and faces* GERALD.) Gerry, I'm sorry about this, but it's not the slightest use getting annoyed with me.

GERALD. No. I'm sorry. (*He moves to the* R. *end of the settee and sits.*) Tell me what he said.

PHILIP. Well, the Skinner episode upset him badly.

GERALD. I know it did.

PHILIP. And you know as well as I do there've been other incidents. The last time you both dined at his house, for instance.

GERALD. You were there.

PHILIP. I was. There's too much talk about your wife, and it's getting worse, and the old man doesn't like it.

GERALD. Does he think I enjoy it ?

PHILIP (*taking a step towards* GERALD). Gerry, can't you persuade her to go into one of these—homes for a bit ?

GERALD. Where do you think she was when she was supposed to be in Italy last year ?

PHILIP (*turning back to the fire*). And it did no good, eh ?

GERALD. She was worse when she came out.

PHILIP (*after a pause*). Do you know there was a scene in the bar of the Adelphi last night ?

GERALD (*looking up*). No ?

PHILIP. Babs was there after the racing, with Donovan and Neumann and that crowd. I gather she was lucky not to find herself at the police station.

GERALD. When did you hear this ?

PHILIP. At lunch time. I've no doubt old Carter heard it too.

GERALD. I've no doubt he did.

PHILIP. Did you know she was up there with Donovan ?

GERALD. She's not. She's staying with Pinkie, but Donovan drove her up. Somebody's got to drive her now she's lost her licence.

PHILIP (*cautiously*). Donovan's not got a very good name.

GERALD. I stopped trying to choose her friends a long time ago.

PHILIP (*moving a step towards* GERALD). Did you ever think you might be able to divorce her ? (*He waits.*)

(GERALD *does not answer.*)

(*He sits in the chair above the fire.*) Look here, Gerry, I know you hate talking about your wife, and so do I, but after all we've been friends for a good many years, and I don't want to see her ruin your life. All I'm suggesting is that you let me find out whether you have grounds for divorce, and if you have, let me start proceedings.

(*There is no answer from* GERALD.)

(*After a pause.*) Well ?

(GERALD *rises.*)

GERALD. I'm sorry, Philip. (*He moves below the table* R. *of the settee.*) I'll think it over and let you know.

PHILIP. Believe me, it's the only sensible course.

GERALD (*going up* C., *and crossing above the settee to the back of* PHILIP'S *chair*). I daresay, old chap. I'll let you know. Have another drink. (*He takes* PHILIP'S *empty glass and goes to the drinks table.*)

PHILIP. Thanks. Anyone else coming to dinner ?

GERALD. No, just ourselves. (*He fills the glass.*) I'd like to go into that Cardiff business after dinner.

PHILIP. I've brought the papers. It's all pretty straight-forward but I still think you're taking a risk.

GERALD. The ships are worth more than we're paying.

PHILIP. No one's buying ships.

GERALD (*coming down between the settee and the arm-chair*). Well, that's the moment to buy, isn't it ? (*He gives the glass to* PHILIP.)

PHILIP. Oh well, I wouldn't try to teach you your business. You're a born gambler, but a lucky one.

GERALD. I don't call it gambling. I pick the odds on chances and back them at even money. I'm bound to win in the end.

PHILIP. A very specious argument. I won't bother to point out the fallacy. (*He puts his glass on the table above the fire.*)

GERALD. No, don't, you'd never cure me.

(MORTON *enters up* L.)

MORTON (*announcing*). Miss Penrose.

(JOYCE PENROSE *comes in. She is a striking-looking and attractive girl of twenty-six, beautifully dressed in clothes which suggest that she has just come from a party. She carries a bag and a pair of gloves.*)

GERALD. Oh, Joyce.

(MORTON *goes out.*)

JOYCE (*up* L.C.). Hullo, Gerry. Good evening, Philip.

PHILIP (*rising*). Good evening, Joyce. (*He stands with his back to the fire.*)

JOYCE. Am I in the way ? Are you two talking business ? (*She comes down below the* L. *end of the settee.*)

PHILIP. No, but Gerald will if he gets a chance ! You stay here.

GERALD (*going to the drinks table*). Philip hates talking business out of hours. Sherry or gin ?

JOYCE (*sitting on the settee*, R. *end*). Sherry, please. A small one. I've not come to stay.

PHILIP. Well, you'd be surprised if you knew how many people expect legal advice in return for a whisky and soda.

GERALD (*coming down* R. *of the settee with a glass*). And how few get it from Philip !

JOYCE. Advice—that's just what I've come for, (*to* PHILIP) but I'm hoping to get it free . . . oh no, from Gerry.

(PHILIP *sits in the arm-chair below the fire.*)

GERALD. Well, I'll do my best. (*He hands her the glass.*) You're looking very smart. Have you been to a party ?

JOYCE. I've been to the Cordreys',

GERALD. Tea-party ?

JOYCE. No—this. (*She holds up her glass.*) Oughtn't you and Babs to have been there ?

GERALD. Oh, Lord !

JOYCE. You'd have been very popular. Everybody was hunting round for someone who wasn't at Aintree yesterday, so that they could tell them all about it.

GERALD. Well, here's your chance—you tell Philip and me.

JOYCE. It was great fun. Of course it *poured*—it poured all day —the wettest National for thirty-seven years. But at least the fog held off till the racing was over, and the going just suited Jackaroo. How did the funeral go ?

GERALD. Well, funerals seldom go with much of a swing. (*He crosses to the fireplace.*) It was the wettest for thirty-nine years, and the going didn't suit anyone.

JOYCE. It was a shame—everyone missed you. I saw Babs, just for a second.

GERALD. Yes, I let her off. Funerals aren't much in her line.

JOYCE. Where is she ?

GERALD. Babs ? She's not back yet.

JOYCE (*in surprise*). Not back ?

GERALD. No, I wasn't expecting her.

JOYCE (*puzzled*). But . . .

GERALD. She's staying with Pinkie.

JOYCE. I thought . . .

GERALD (*quickly and firmly*). Did you see Pinkie ?

JOYCE. Yes, of course I did—you can't miss Pinkie, even at Aintree. She was in crashing form. She had her usual enormous house-party.

GERALD. Yes, she never knows half of them, but they all answer to " Dearie."

JOYCE. And everyone calls her Pinkie—even the bookies do.

PHILIP. She's a great lad, Pinkie. When her father had the Royal in Liverpool, it was Pinkie who filled the place, and there was never any trouble on a Saturday night when Pinkie was behind the bar.

GERALD (*going to the table above the settee*). No, nor any other night, either. (*He picks up the cigarette box.*)

JOYCE. I never think of her and Babs as sisters, somehow.

(GERALD *takes a cigarette and replaces the box on the table.*)

PHILIP. No, they're not much alike.

GERALD (*coming down* R. *of settee, fidgeting with the cigarette*). Oh, Joyce, you wanted my advice about something. What was it?

JOYCE. Yes, about that mare of Jimmy Hennessy's. I'm thinking of buying her.

GERALD. What, the chestnut?

JOYCE. Yes, Daisybell. I said I'd let him know definitely tomorrow.

GERALD. Well, my advice is don't touch her.

JOYCE. Oh, but Gerry, she's just what I want. She ran second in the lightweights at the Bramham Moor last year.

GERALD. Yes, and no one but Jimmy would have got her round. Last time he had her out with hounds, she jumped on the Master. She'd pull your arms out.

JOYCE. I don't think so. Jimmy says she——

GERALD. No, Joyce, you mustn't buy Daisybell, she's not safe.

(MORTON *enters up* L.)

JOYCE. All right——

MORTON (*announcing*). Mr. Darling.

(BUNS DARLING *comes in. He is a young forty ; rather chubby-faced, very pleased with himself, very immaculate in a dinner-jacket. In his early twenties he decided that a poker face is effective. His expression seldom changes, and he never smiles.* MORTON *goes out.*)

GERALD (*surprised*). Hullo, Buns.

BUNS. Evening, Gerry. Hullo, Joyce.

JOYCE. Hello, Buns.

BUNS (*coming down to the fire*). Evening, Balfour. (*He stands, with his back to the fire, on one leg, shaking the other leg in front of the flames.*)

PHILIP. Evening.

BUNS. Filthy night, isn't it?

GERALD. Horrible. You look a bit wet.

BUNS (*feeling his trousers*). I am rather—I walked over.

(GERALD *lights his cigarette.*)

Silly of me. I ought to have rung up Renton's and got hold of a car.

JOYCE. What's happened to yours?

BUNS. Well, that's rather a long story—I left it up in Liverpool last night. (*He feels his trousers again.*) I say, you know, I am a bit wet about the hocks. D'you think your man could give me a rub down ?

GERALD. Of course. Just ring that bell will you ?

(BUNS *rings the bell below the fireplace.*)

BUNS. Well, old man, what happened to you yesterday ? I hear you missed the race.

GERALD. Yes, I had to go to old Mrs. Carter's funeral.

BUNS. Good Lord ! (*He sits in the arm-chair above the fire.*) They ought to close the cemeteries on National Day. Saw you in the distance at the Cordreys, Joyce. Rather a good party, I thought. Everyone seemed to be there.

JOYCE. Except Gerry and Philip !

GERALD. I don't like cocktails, do you Philip ? I like to know what I'm drinking——

(MORTON *opens door up* L.)

PHILIP. So do I and I like to drink it sitting down.

(MORTON *enters.*)

GERALD. Oh Morton, do you think you could get a cloth and dry Mr. Darling a bit ?

BUNS (*rising*). No, no, we won't make a mess of your carpet, we'll do it outside.

(*The clock strikes eight.* BUNS *and* MORTON *go out up* L.)

PHILIP (*rising*). Has that fellow just dropped in to dry his pants ?

GERALD (*moving upstage*). That's what I'm wondering. (*He crosses above the settee to the* L. *end.*)

PHILIP. Or has he come to dinner ?

JOYCE. Weren't you expecting him ?

GERALD. I certainly wasn't. D'you think he's come on the wrong night, or to the wrong house ? If it's just the wrong house, it's easy—we dry him and pass him on.

JOYCE. If he knows where he's dining !

PHILIP (*crossing below the settee to* C.). O-oh, he's dining here, you'll find. He doesn't make that sort of mistake—he's a professional. He hasn't dined in his own house for years. I doubt if he has a knife and fork of his own. (*He continues his move to the desk.*)

GERALD. Well, I didn't ask him.

JOYCE. Perhaps Babs did, and forgot all about it.

PHILIP. That's like enough, I think. Must I stay ?

GERALD (*sitting in the arm-chair above the fire*). Yes, of course you must stay—why not ?

PHILIP. He's not my idea of a happy evening.

GERALD. Oh, he's all right, he's a type.

PHILIP. Why do they call him Buns?

GERALD. Haven't the slightest idea, but it suits him down to the ground.

JOYCE. One calls him Buns instinctively.

PHILIP (*picking up the newspaper*). My instincts don't work that way.

GERALD. You can't call him Darling.

PHILIP. I do. (*He puts down the newspaper.*) But I make it perfectly clear that it is *not* a term of endearment. (*He sits in the arm-chair at* R.C.)

(MORTON *opens the door up* L. *and lets* BUNS *in. He then goes out again.*)

GERALD (*rising*). All right, now?

BUNS. Better, I think.

GERALD (*going up* L. *of the settee to the drinks table*). Well, having dried your outside, what about wetting your inside? Sherry or gin?

BUNS (*coming down to the fire*). May I stick to whisky for the moment? (*He stands with his back to the fire.*) I say, Gerry, that man of yours, wasn't he with Archie Daubeney?

GERALD (*pouring out whisky*). Morton? Yes. Why?

BUNS. I thought he was. It's always worried me a bit—knew I'd seen him before somewhere, and to-night I suddenly spotted him. The old subconscious, I suppose.

GERALD. What about it?

BUNS. You know Archie sacked him for selling his wine?

GERALD (*coming down to the fire with a glass*). I never believed that yarn. For one thing, nobody'd buy Daubeney's wine.

PHILIP. That's very true.

(BUNS *takes the glass.*)

GERALD. Daubeney behaved damn badly. He had no proof— he chucked the old man out of the house and refused him a reference. (*He sits on the* L. *arm of the settee.*)

PHILIP. So you took him on. Well, well.

GERALD. Why not? I've never regretted it. I've had him nearly five years, and he suits me down to the ground.

BUNS. Well, I hope he won't let you down that's all ; but I always say that's one rule I never break—I never take on a servant without a reference. Yes, yes, I know what you're going to say— intuition and all that—one look at a man's face—but I don't take any chances. I remember a fellow once——

GERALD (*interrupting*). I say, Buns, I hope it's not a rude question, but have you come to dinner?

BUNS. Well, naturally. (*He puts his glass on the mantelpiece.*) Aren't you expecting me? (*He takes out an engagement book and finds the place in it.*)

GERALD. Frankly, no—but I don't say we'll turn you out into the cold wet night.

BUNS (*going to* GERALD *and showing him the book*). Yes, here we are. Saturday the 28th. Dine Babs.

GERALD (*rising*). Oh, Babs asked you ; oh, that's fine then. (*He goes to the bell.*)

BUNS. But didn't she tell you ? Where is she ?

(GERALD *rings the bell.*)

GERALD. She's not back yet, she's staying with Pinkie. (*He sits in the arm-chair below the fire.*)

BUNS. Good Lord ! . . . Of course, I saw her at Aintree yesterday, but she said she was coming back to-day.

GERALD. Well, she hasn't.

BUNS. Good Lord ! (*He sits in the arm-chair above the fire.*) As a matter of fact, I put her on to Jackaroo, and I think she had a pretty good win. Then I ran into her again in the evening at the Adelphi, and she said, " Come and dine to-morrow." Sort of *quid pro quo*, I imagine.

GERALD. Well, I hope there's an adequate *quid*.

JOYCE. Gerry, why not make a job of it, and ask me too ?

PHILIP. That's a good idea, that'll make a bridge four.

(MORTON *enters up* L.)

GERALD. That's a very good idea. Let's just see if there's any food, shall we ? Morton, d'you think Mrs. Sykes can spread dinner a bit, and make it cover four ?

MORTON. Yes, sir.

(PHILIP *rises.*)

GERALD. Good. Well, Miss Penrose and Mr. Darling——

PHILIP (*cutting in*). Morton, you say " Yes, sir " very confidently, but have you any grounds for that assertion ?

MORTON. Yes, sir. I have already asked Mrs. Sykes. I foresaw the possibility, sir.

JOYCE. One to Morton. (*She rises. She leaves her bag and gloves on the settee.*) May I telephone ? (*She crosses to the desk and sits in the chair.*)

GERALD. Yes, rather, do.

PHILIP (*coming downstage of the table* R. *of the settee, to* MORTON). Well, I'm the only guest who was expected, Morton. I trust you'll remember that when you're helping us.

(JOYCE *dials a number.*)

MORTON. I will bear it in mind, sir. (*To* GERALD.) Mrs. Sykes is sorry, sir, but she is afraid that, owing to this, dinner may be a little late.

GERALD. That's all right. Tell her there's no hurry.

MORTON. Thank you, sir.

(MORTON *goes out.*)

GERALD (*rising*). The drink'll hold out, anyway. Buns ? (*He takes the glass from the mantelpiece.*)

BUNS. Thanks.

(PHILIP *sits on the settee*, R. *end.*)

GERALD. Joyce ? (*He goes up to the drinks table.*)

JOYCE. Please.

GERALD. What have you done with your car, Buns ? Smashed it up ?

BUNS (*rising and standing with his back to the fire*). Good Lord, no. No, I went up in it yesterday, of course, and then—Shh—shh. (*He indicates* JOYCE *telephoning.*)

JOYCE. Is that Chambers ? . . . Miss Joyce speaking. Will you please tell my father I won't be in to dinner ? . . . Thank you. (*She rings off.*)

BUNS (*going upstage, above the* L. *end of the settee*). Well, and then, to be perfectly honest, I didn't feel like driving it home last night. Fact is, I'd had a pretty good day, and then I met Squeaker Bullen in the Adelphi—you know Squeaker ?

GERALD (*coming down to the fireplace*). No, I'm afraid I don't. (*He gives* BUNS *his drink as he passes him.*)

BUNS (*following* GERALD *down*). Old Combermere's son—was in the Tins. Well, one bottle rather led to another,

(GERALD *picks up* PHILIP'S *glass from the table above the fire and turns* L. *He finds himself face to face with* BUNS. BUNS *sidesteps.*)

and to cut a long story short, by the time I got into the car, things weren't as steady as they might have been.

(GERALD *crosses* BUNS. BUNS *follows a couple of steps*. GERALD *continues below the settee and up* C. *to the drinks table.* BUNS *finds himself left at the* L. *end of the settee.*)

I nearly chanced it, but the fog was pretty thick and I thought, no. This simply isn't good enough, I thought, train for you, my lad. (*He sits on the stool* L.C.)

GERALD (*filling the glass*). Very sensible of you. (*He comes down* R. *of the settee.*)

BUNS. So I came home by train, like a good boy, and there's the Railton up in Liverpool. I suppose someone can give me a lift home ?

GERALD (*giving the glass to* PHILIP). Oh, yes, rather—Philip'd love to.

PHILIP (*not at all pleased*). I will.

(GERALD *goes up to the drinks table again.*)

BUNS. Thanks. Mind you, by the time I got home, I was almost sorry I hadn't chanced it in the car. Pea-soup fog all the way—the twelve forty-two didn't get here till half past one, and then it stuck on the level crossing. I got out and walked in the end, everyone was doing it. (*He rises and moves above the* L. *end of the settee.*) Oh, of course, you were on that train, Gerry—what time did you get home ?

(GERALD *spills some soda-water.* *He looks up slowly.*)

GERALD. I ?

BUNS. Well, you were, weren't you ? I saw you on the platform in Liverpool.

GERALD. Not me. I wasn't in Liverpool at all yesterday. (*He comes down to the* L. *arm of the settee and sits.*)

BUNS. Oh, I know you weren't at Aintree. No, I thought you'd gone up for a party or something in the evening. Well, all I can say is you must have a double.

PHILIP. Perhaps it was due to your own doubles.

BUNS. What ? Ha ! ha! ha! Well, I've owned up I *was* a bit shot away, and I hardly got more than a back view, but I could have sworn it was you.

GERALD. No, I have a very ordinary back.

(*The front door bell rings.*)

JOYCE. Listen . . . there's the bell ! Someone else is arriving.

BUNS (*coming down to the fireplace*). Babs, I expect—bound to be. (*He puts his glass on the mantelpiece.*)

JOYCE. No, she'd come straight in—wouldn't she, Gerry ?

GERALD. Yes, of course she would. (*He puts out his cigarette in the ashtray on the table behind the settee and puts his glass on the table.*)

PHILIP. I wish I'd brought sandwiches.

(MORTON *enters up* L.)

MORTON (*announcing*). Mrs. Collins.

(PHILIP, GERALD *and* JOYCE *rise.* PHILIP *breaks* R. *towards* JOYCE. *He puts his glass on the table* R. *of the settee.* PINKIE COLLINS *comes in.* *She is between thirty-five and forty ; stout and a little vulgar, but lively, natural, and thoroughly good-hearted.* MORTON *goes out.*)

GERALD. Pinkie ! (*He moves above the* L. *end of the settee.*)

PINKIE. Gerry ! (*She gives him a hug and a kiss.*) I'm frightfully late—I know I am. Couldn't help it—I told Babs I would be. (*She comes down to the fireplace.*) Hullo, Joyce. Hullo, Buns. (*She goes to* PHILIP.) Philip, my dear ! (*She kisses him.*)

PHILIP. Pinkie my dear, you're the only woman in the world who kisses me.

PINKIE. Oh, bless the boy ! Here's another. (*She kisses him again.*)

PHILIP. Have you brought Babs with you ?

(GERALD *comes down* L. *of the stool at* L.C.)

PINKIE. Babs, dear ? No.

GERALD. Where is she, then ?

(PINKIE *turns to* GERALD. *She looks nonplussed.*)

She's staying with you, isn't she ?

PINKIE (*thoughtfully and rather slowly*). Oh, yes—yes, of course, only she left this morning . . . or was it this morning ? I've had such a houseful coming and going . . . Or was it yesterday ?

GERALD (*going up to the end of the settee*). Was she coming home ?

PINKIE. She said she was. You mean she hasn't arrived ? (*She goes up* C. *to the* R. *end of the settee.*)

GERALD. No.

PINKIE. And she hasn't rung up ?

GERALD. No.

PINKIE. Well ! . . . Gerry, you don't think anything's happened —an accident or anything ?

GERALD. Oh, no, we'd have heard.

PINKIE (*her hand to her head*). Now let me think. She said she . . . what's to-day.

ALL (*except* BUNS). Saturday.

BUNS. Saturday !

PINKIE. That's right, and yesterday was . . .

BUNS. Friday !

PINKIE. That's right, it's Saturday. And Babs said she . . . Oh, well, I don't know what can have happened, but you know what Babs is, she's a bit vague sometimes. There were lots of them all leaving together, I expect someone asked her to stay the night. (*She crosses above the settee to the arm-chair above the fire.*) That's what's happened—she'll roll up tomorrow. (*She sinks into the chair.*) Well, isn't this nice ? My word, I'm tired ! I've had a hectic week. Got a little drink, dearie ?

GERALD. Yes, rather, what will you have ? Sherry ? (*He goes up to the drinks table.*)

PINKIE. No dear, gin !

PHILIP (*moving up* R. *of the table behind the settee*). You'll stay to dinner, won't you, Pinkie ?

(*Everybody laughs.* PINKIE *looks astonished.*)

GERALD (*coming down to* R. *of* PINKIE). Of course you will. Don't pay any attention to Philip. (*He gives her the drink.*)

PINKIE. I told Babs I'd be late . . . Oh ! . . . you don't mean to say you weren't expecting me ?

(GERALD *sits on* L. *arm of settee. Everybody laughs again.* BUNS *crosses to the settee and sits at the* R. *end.*)

GERALD. Well, as a matter of fact, Babs didn't let me know.

PINKIE. Oh, my dear, how awful ! Oh, this is naughty of her !

BUNS. She asked me, too.

PINKIE. But Gerry, I . . .

PHILIP. Pinkie, my dear, we can discuss it later. You go and wash your hands like a good girl, and let's get in to dinner before the crowd gets any thicker.

PINKIE. But, good heavens, I've brought a suit-case ! I'm staying till Wednesday !

GERALD (*rising and moving towards* PINKIE). Better and better. We never see half enough of you.

PINKIE. Isn't he a dear boy ! (*She puts her glass on the table above the fire.*)

(PHILIP *moves to the stool up* R.)

GERALD. All the same, you had better wash if you want to. Philip's in a difficult mood.   I'll come and see where Morton's put you. (*He goes to the door.*)

(PINKIE *rises and starts for the door up* L.)

JOYCE (*rising*). Gerry, can I take my things off ? (*She moves to the* R. *end of the settee.*)

(BUNS *rises and hands* JOYCE *her bag and gloves.*)

GERALD. Yes, of course—come along. (*He opens the door.*)

(JOYCE *crosses above the settee to the door up* L.)

PINKIE. Well, I must say, I do feel awful !

(PINKIE *goes out.*)

JOYCE. Now why ? I invited myself.

(JOYCE *goes out.*)

GERALD. Yes, and look at Buns—he doesn't mind a bit.

(PHILIP *picks up a magazine from the stool up* R. *and comes down to the desk.* GERALD *goes out.*)

BUNS (*hurt ; moving to the fireplace*). Well, I wrote it down in my book. I must say it's a bit awkward, Babs making a mistake like this. Mind you, between you and me, I'm not altogether surprised.

(PHILIP *takes the magazine from the desk.*)

PHILIP (*grunting in a surly way*). Hmph ? (*He crosses slowly down* C.)

BUNS. Well, you know what Babs is at the best of times, and last night in the Adelphi she and that chap Donovan—by Jove, they were hitting it a crack ! All the same, she said she was coming home to-day. What do you make of it ?

PHILIP. You heard Pinkie say she's probably gone to stay with someone. (*He comes below the* R. *end of the settee.*)

BUNS. Were you watching Pinkie ? (*There is no answer.*) Well, I was. You don't often see Pinkie rattled, but that's what she was just now—she was rattled. She expected to find Babs here,

(PHILIP *sits on the settee*, R. *end. He drops one magazine on the settee above him so that he is half sitting on it ; he reads the other.)*

and it was a bit of a shock when she didn't. And if you ask me who Babs is staying with, I fancy I'd get it in one. (*He takes a step towards* PHILIP.) She's with Donovan. (*He pauses, but* PHILIP *says nothing.*) You know, I think someone ought to say a word to old Gerry. (*He turns back to the fire.*)

PHILIP (*reading*). Try it.

BUNS (*turning*). Good Lord, no—not me ! No, I thought you might take it on, you're a pal of his. Yes, I know what you're going to say—that old Gerry's no fool. I know that, but the husband's always the last person to hear of it.

PHILIP (*still reading*). Hmph !

BUNS. Then look at the way Babs is hitting the bottle—good Lord ! . . . I'm the last person to object to a woman having a drink or two, but really (*He moves to the settee and sits,* L. *end.*) . . . Last night in the Adelphi—she was like a madwoman ! They chucked her out in the end, but I thought they'd have to send for the police. I don't suppose you heard about that ?

PHILIP. Hmph.

BUNS. Well, she came in with Donovan at about——

PHILIP (*not looking up*). I said I *had* heard about it.

BUNS. Oh ! (*He is undeterred.*) When I saw Gerry on the train last night, I thought he'd gone up to bail her out, or something.

PHILIP (*still not looking up*). You heard Gerry say he wasn't in Liverpool last night.

BUNS. Yes, so he did. Funny thing, I could have sworn I saw him. Not sure I believe him now, you know—may have had a date he didn't want people to know about—yes, yes, I know what you're going to say——

PHILIP (*viciously*). I doubt it.

BUNS. I beg your pardon ?

PHILIP (*lowering the magazine at last*). I say I doubt if you know what I was going to say. I was going to point out that that's the third slanderous statement you've made in the last two minutes.

BUNS. Oh, my dear chap !

PHILIP. And it hardly improves matters that all three were aimed at your host and hostess.

BUNS. But, my dear fellow, I'm only saying what everybody knows is true !

PHILIP. When you find yourself in court, you'll discover that doesn't help.

BUNS. Good lord !

(PHILIP *returns ostentatiously to his paper.* BUNS *is obviously agitated, but after a few moments he pulls himself together. He snatches the magazine from under* PHILIP.)

BUNS (*elaborately*). Excuse me. (*He rises and goes to the fireplace.*)
(PHILIP *grunts.*)

PHILIP (*suddenly and impatiently*). Devil take it ! What's the time ? (*He looks at the clock on the mantelpiece.*)

BUNS (*glancing at the clock*). Seventeen minutes past eight—if that's not a slanderous statement. (*He sits in the arm-chair below the fire.*)

(JOYCE *enters up* L. *She has removed her coat.*)

JOYCE (*coming* L. *of the settee*). Pinkie's just coming. (*She sits on the* L. *arm.*)

PHILIP. And about time, too.

JOYCE. There's a lovely foody smell in the hall.

PHILIP. That was there when I arrived.

(PINKIE *enters up* L. GERALD *follows her in. He closes the door.*)

PINKIE (*coming round the* L. *end of the settee*). Well, I am sorry to keep you all. My, but I'm tired ! (*She sits on the settee.*) Thank God there's not another National for a year !

(GERALD *crosses upstage to the chair* R.C.)

PHILIP. Who did you have staying with you ?

PINKIE. Everyone who's ever had a horse in Bertie's stables for a week.

GERALD. How many's that Pinkie ?

PINKIE. Never counted them, dearie, they never stayed still for a minute.

(MORTON *enters up* L.)

MORTON. Dinner is served, Sir.

(PHILIP, BUNS *and* JOYCE *rise.*)

GERALD. Good. (*He counts his guests.*) And then—one, two, three, four, five—poker instead of bridge, I think.

PINKIE (*rising and going upstage past* JOYCE). Not for me, thanks —not tonight. I'm going to put my feet up.

(*The telephone rings.*)

That's Babs !

(GERALD *goes to the telephone and lifts the receiver.* PHILIP *picks up his glass and stands* R. *of the table* R. *of the settee.* BUNS *moves upstage to* JOYCE. *Everybody watches* GERALD.)

GERALD (*tensely*). Chillington 63. (*He pauses.*) Oh, hello Kathleen ! . . . Babs ? No, she's not back, yet . . . I haven't the slightest idea . . . yes, I will as soon as she gets back . . . good-bye ! (*He puts down the receiver.*) Come on, dinner. (*To* PHILIP.) Bring that in with you. (*He crosses up* L.)

(PHILIP *moves up* L.)

PINKIE (*going to the door*). Don't worry, Gerry, she'll turn up tomorrow.

(PINKIE *goes out up* L. JOYCE *and* BUNS *follow her out.*)

GERALD. Yes, I'm sure she will.

(PHILIP *and* GERALD *go out talking.*)

CURTAIN.

SCENE 2.

SCENE —*The same. About two and a half hours later.*

A card table has been placed below the arm-chair R.C. R. *of it is the chair from down* R., *and* L. *of it is the chair from the desk. The stool from up* R. *has been placed below it.* GERALD *is facing the audience in the chair* R.C. ; L. *of him, in the desk chair, is* PHILIP ; *and* R. *of him is* BUNS ; JOYCE, *his partner, is sitting on the stool.* PINKIE, *with her feet up on the settee, her head at the upstage end, is sound asleep. A newspaper has fallen from her hand.*

As the CURTAIN *rises* GERALD *plays a card.* PHILIP *follows quickly.* JOYCE *rises and goes up to the table behind the settee.* GERALD *plays quickly from dummy.* JOYCE *takes a cigarette and lights it.* BUNS *thinks for a moment and then plays.* GERALD *takes the trick and plays again.* JOYCE *moves to* GERALD'S L. *and watches.* PHILIP *plays quickly and* GERALD *follows quickly from dummy.* BUNS *thinks long and deeply.*

GERALD. Now, just one more club. Known as a " squeeze," Buns, very painful.

(BUNS *plays.*)

That makes my hearts both good. (*He puts the remainder of his hand down.*)

(PHILIP *and* BUNS *throw in their cards.*)

JOYCE. When you called five hearts, I must put you with the ace.

PHILIP. If my partner hadn't doubled, you'd have had to play for the drop.

BUNS. I had to double. I had four trumps to the queen, and the ace of clubs.

PHILIP. And your double told him you had just that.

GERALD (*reprovingly*). Now, now, now, Philip. That's 360 below, 500 for the rubber, and 750 for the little slam. That's seventeen hundred in all.

JOYCE. I can't add up. (*She comes downstage behind* PHILIP *to his* L.)

BUNS. You trust Gerry.

PHILIP. Seventeen it is. (*Muttering.*) Seventeen, thirteen, seven—thirty-seven. Darling and I owe thirty-seven shillings each. (*He puts his hand in his pocket and takes out two one pound notes.*)

BUNS. That's right.

GERALD. A nice cheap evening for you, Philip.

PHILIP (*offering the notes to* JOYCE). I'd sooner pay you, Joyce.

JOYCE (*taking them*). I'm sorry, I'm afraid I've got no change. I warned you I was playing on tick.

PHILIP (*taking his money back quickly from her hand*). Then I'll pay Gerald. (*He puts the notes on the table in front of* GERALD.)

GERALD. Trusting, isn't he ? (*He takes a one pound note and two ten shilling notes from* BUNS.) I've got plenty of change. Now what about drinks ?

(BUNS *and* PHILIP *rise and go up to the drinks table.*)

(*He hands some money to* JOYCE.) Help yourselves. (*He rises.*) Joyce ?

(JOYCE *crosses to the desk and puts the money in her bag.* BUNS *and* PHILIP *help themselves to drinks and then stand below the drinks table.* BUNS *on the* R. GERALD *goes to the drinks table.*)

JOYCE. Plain soda, please. (*She puts her bag back on the desk.*)

GERALD. Oh, have some of this stuff. Lemonade, I think.

JOYCE (*going up* R. *of the card table to the alcove*). All right, I'll try some of that. (*She stands* C. *in the alcove.*)

(GERALD *fills a glass with lemonade.*)

BUNS. I must say I was holding foul cards all night.

(PHILIP *crosses in front of* BUNS *to the back of the chair* R.C. GERALD *turns to* JOYCE.)

JOYCE (*taking the glass from* GERALD). Gerry had all the cards. (*She moves down* L. *of the settee.*)

GERALD (*standing in front of the radio*). A good player often gives that impression.

PHILIP. You had the devil's own luck. Everything lay right for you all night.

GERALD. That's called intelligent deduction from the bidding. (*He moves down to the settee,* L. *end.*)

BUNS (*moving to the* L. *of the table above the settee*). You know, Balfour, I still think I was right to double that last hand—don't you, really ?

PHILIP (*moving to* R. *of the table above the settee*). Since you ask me—no, Darling.

(*They all look down at* PINKIE *as she lies asleep.*)

BUNS. By jove, flat out, isn't she ?

PHILIP. I wish I slept as peacefully as that.

GERALD. She must have a nice clear conscience.

JOYCE (*sitting on the stool* L.C.). She had a frightful nightmare just now.

GERALD. Oh, you mean that little yelp she gave ? Oh, I don't think so—I think she was chasing something in her sleep.

JOYCE. It's a shame ! I'd hate to wake up and find four people staring down at me.

GERALD. Well, break things up a bit, and I'll wake her.

(BUNS *crosses to* R. *above the desk.* PHILIP *breaks to the chair* R.C. JOYCE *rises and stands on the hearthrug.*)

(*He tweaks her nose—no effect.*) PINKIE ! ! !

JOYCE. No, Gerry, you'll have to shake her.

GERALD (*gently*). Pinkie ! (*No effect.*) Pinkie, dear. (*He puts a hand on her shoulder and shakes her gently.*)

PINKIE. Oh ! . . . Hullo ! . . . Was I asleep ?

GERALD (*picking up the newspaper*). No, no, you were reading *The Times.*

PINKIE. Oh, no, I wasn't. (*She yawns and stretches.*) I had a lovely little snooze.

(JOYCE *sits in the arm-chair down* L.)

PHILIP. We heard you.

PINKIE. I *wasn't* snoring. Oh, heavens, I wish I was in bed ! What's the time ? (*She slides her legs off the settee and sits up at the* R. *end.*)

GERALD. Just after eleven.

PINKIE. What time's breakfast ?

GERALD. As late as you like, and you can have it in bed.

PINKIE. Bless you !

GERALD. A little drink ? (*He goes up to the drinks table.*)

PINKIE, Yes, please, just a weak one.

PHILIP. Well, Gerry, I don't have breakfast in bed. I'm going home. (*He crosses above the settee to up* L.)

GERALD. All right, old man. We didn't talk much business, did we ?

PHILIP (*turning by the door*). Good night, Pinkie—Good night, Joyce. (*To* GERALD.) I'll come and see you on Monday about the Cardiff business.

GERALD (*coming down* R. *of the settee*). Right-o. I'll ring up and fix a time. (*He hands the drink to* PINKIE.)

BUNS. I say, Balfour. (*He crosses hastily to* PHILIP.) You said you'd drop me, didn't you ?

PHILIP (*turning and going out*). With pleasure.

(PHILIP *goes out.*)

BUNS. Good night, Joyce—good night, Pinkie.

(PINKIE *and* JOYCE *murmur* " *Good night.*" BUNS *goes out.*)

GERALD (*following* BUNS). I'll see you out, Morton's gone to bed. (*To* PINKIE.) I'll be back in a minute.

(GERALD *goes out. He shuts the door.*)

PINKIE. That little snooze did me good. (*She rises and moves to the stool* L.C.) I suppose that sister of mine didn't ring up, did she ?

JOYCE. No.

PINKIE. I can't think what's happened to her. Oh, well, I suppose she'll roll up to-morrow. (*She dismisses the subject and goes to the fire.*) Have a nice game, dear ? I hope you won.

JOYCE (*rising and crossing up to the drinks table*). I did. Gerry and I took them on. We won every rubber. (*She puts her glass on the table.*)

PINKIE. Bertie always says Gerry's the only really first-class bridge player he knows.

JOYCE. Don't tell Gerry that. I always say he overcalls his hand. (*She returns to the* L. *end of the table above the settee.*)

PINKIE. Oh, he's a bit of a gambler over everything, but then look at the way things come out right for him. When he married Babs, you know, he was a clerk on four pounds a week.

JOYCE. I know.

PINKIE (*sitting in the arm-chair above the fire*). My old dad didn't like the idea, I can tell you. He was doing pretty well out of the Royal in those days, and " My daughter's not going to marry a clerk on four pounds a week," he said. In the end, of course, Gerry talked the old man round, and six years later he bought the Royal, just to try to help my dad.

JOYCE (*coming down* L. *of the settee*). Did you know Gerry's father ? (*She sits on the settee,* L. *end.*)

PINKIE. No, but Bertie did. Bertie started under him. Bertie always said old Coates was the finest trainer in the North. It wasn't his fault he went down, he just had a run of bad luck, but it came at a bad time for Gerry.

JOYCE. I suppose he was lucky really to get the chance of a job in old Carter's office.

PINKIE. O-ho, old Carter jumped at him. He thought he'd got a cheap clerk and a free jockey. " But you watch me," he said. " I'm going into that office at the bottom and I'm coming out at the top." And so he has.

JOYCE. My father says there wasn't an amateur rider in England to touch Gerry.

PINKIE. Nor a pro either. You saw him win on Dutch Prince.

JOYCE. No, I didn't—I wish I had.

PINKIE (*rising and putting her glass on the fireside arm of the chair down* L.). I never saw anything like it. He broke a leather three fences from home, and then the old horse pecked badly over the last fence. (*She stands with her back to the fire.*) How Gerry held him up, I don't know ! He won by half a length from Kerry Battle . . . Oh, and the party we threw at the Adelphi that night !

(GERALD *comes in up* L.)

GERALD. Poor old Philip. (*He comes down* L. *of the settee.*) He doesn't suffer fools gladly. He's gone off rumbling queer legal oaths at Buns, like a volcano about to erupt. (*He sits on the* L. *arm of the settee.*)

PINKIE. Are your ears burning, dearie ? I've been telling Joyce about your win on Dutch Prince.

GERALD. Poor old Prince ! It was a shame.

JOYCE. What was ?

GERALD. He carried me all the way round Aintree, and I never realised what he suffered until after the party that night. I had to carry Pinkie up to bed.

PINKIE. Go on with you. But you can carry me up now if you like. (*She moves above the stool* L.C.) Will you think me rude, dear, if I hit the hay ?

JOYCE (*rising*). No, of course not. And I must be getting home. (*She crosses to the desk and collects her bag.*)

PINKIE. Don't do that, Joyce, I'll feel I'm driving you away. Gerry, I do think it's queer about Babs.

GERALD (*slipping off the arm of the settee and moving to the fireplace*). If she really meant to come back to-night, it is.

PINKIE (*to* JOYCE). Did you see her at Aintree ?

JOYCE (*moving below the stool* R.C.). Yesterday I did—just for a moment.

PINKIE. Did she say anything ?—about her plans, I mean ?

JOYCE. As a matter of fact, she did. She told me she was coming home to-day.

PINKIE. I'm certain she meant to come home. (*She turns to* GERALD.) I'm worried, Gerry—I can't help it. I've got a feeling there's something wrong—an accident or something.

GERALD. Oh, rot, darling, we'd have heard.

PINKIE. Yes, I suppose we would. (*She moves to him.*) But look here, dear, I wouldn't let her go driving about with that Donovan, I wouldn't trust him to drive me, not from here to the gate. Oh, well . . . good night, dear. (*She kisses him.*)

GERALD (*going up* L. *to the door*). No, I'm coming up to make sure you've got everything.

PINKIE. Thank you, dear. (*She crosses to* JOYCE *and kisses her.*)

JOYCE. And then I must go.

(PINKIE *crosses downstage towards the fireplace.*)

PINKIE (*turning below the settee ; to* JOYCE). Breakfast in bed as late as I like ! . . . It's nice to be a guest for a change. (*She turns back towards the fireplace and pauses for a moment under the portrait of* BABS.) She *was* pretty when that was painted, wasn't she ? (*She continues up* L. *to the door.*) Oh, well . . . Good night, Joyce dear.

JOYCE. Good night, Pinkie. Sleep well.

PINKIE (*going out*). You give me ten minutes, and you'd have to wake me with a hatchet.

(PINKIE *exits.* GERALD *follows her out.* JOYCE *moves up* C. *and crosses above the settee to up* L. *She comes down* L. *of the settee to the fireplace. She stands for a moment looking up at the portrait. She hears* GERALD *outside the door and turns her back quickly to the fire.* GERALD *enters.*)

JOYCE (*on the defensive*). I won't stay long.

GERALD (*coming down* L. *of the settee*). Stay as long as you can. (*He stands above the stool* L.C.)

JOYCE. Oh, Gerry . . . and you've been telling me to go for the last ten minutes.

GERALD. I have ?

JOYCE. You know you have . . . I heard you.

GERALD. You must have ears like a bat.

JOYCE. Nothing to do with my ears. Why do you want me to go ?

GERALD. Only because it seemed wiser. (*He moves to* JOYCE.)

JOYCE. Gerry, I haven't seen you since Wednesday. It's seemed an awfully long time.

GERALD. Yes, I've thought so, too.

JOYCE (*taking a step towards him*). Need we be so wise ? You keep on making the most impossible rules.

GERALD. No, there's only one rule, and that's only for me . . . to look after you as well as I can till I'm free to marry you.

JOYCE. Does that mean we can't even have five minutes together when we get the chance ?

GERALD (*taking her hand*). It means not doing anything that might start people talking.

JOYCE. There's nothing to talk about.

GERALD. That wouldn't stop them. (*He turns and crosses below the settee.*)

JOYCE. It seems to mean a good deal more than that.

GERALD (*going up* R. *of the settee*). Yes . . . it does. It means keeping you as . . . (*He faces her across the back of the settee,* R. *end.*) uninvolved as possible, in every way, till things clear up for us.

JOYCE (*moving to the settee*). *Uninvolved !* Oh, Gerry, that's just . . . it simply doesn't make sense ! (*She sits on the settee,* R. *end, and leans across the back to him.*) How can I be more involved than I am ? Head over ears, that's what I am . . . head over ears !

GERALD (*leaning over her*). All right, we're both head over ears . . . that's something we can't help. But that's where we stop. Darling, we've had all this, and you know damn well what I mean.

You can make it hard or you can make it easy, but it's got to be the way I say.

JOYCE (*after a pause*). I know you're right . . . I'll make it easy.

GERALD (*breaking away*). I should have said, as easy as you can.

JOYCE. May I stay five minutes longer ?

GERALD. Yes, of course.

(JOYCE *rises and goes to the chair above the fire.*)

JOYCE (*sitting*). A queer evening, wasn't it ?

GERALD. Queer ? . . . You mean Buns and Pinkie turning up like that ?

JOYCE. Yes, perhaps that was it . . . or were we all waiting for Babs ?

GERALD (*moving into the alcove up* C.). It might have been that.

JOYCE. Gerry, what is Babs doing ? Where is she ?

GERALD. I've no idea. (*He looks closely at the picture above the radio.*)

JOYCE. But you said she hadn't been back.

GERALD. She hasn't.

JOYCE. She was here last night.

GERALD (*lightly*). Babs ? No, she wasn't.

JOYCE. But Gerry she was ! I rang up, and she spoke to me.

GERALD (*turning incredulously*). Last night ?

JOYCE. Yes. Do you mean you didn't know she was here ?

GERALD. She wasn't. She didn't leave Pinkie until this morning . . . Pinkie said so.

JOYCE. Yes, I know. But Pinkie . . . didn't seem awfully sure.

GERALD (*coming down* L. *of the settee*). What time did you ring up ? (*He sits on the* L. *arm.*)

(JOYCE *thinks for a moment.*)

JOYCE. About eleven . . . a little after, perhaps.

GERALD. And Babs answered the phone ?

JOYCE. Yes.

GERALD. But I was here the whole evening . . .

JOYCE. Gerry, how extraordinary !

GERALD. Tell me what happened.

JOYCE. Yesterday at Aintree she said she was coming home to-day, so when I got back last night, I . . . thought I'd ring you up.

GERALD. Yes ?

JOYCE. And Babs answered the phone.

GERALD. What did she say ?

JOYCE. She answered . . . She said, ' Hello ? ' I wasn't expecting it, and I just put down the receiver.

GERALD. Was that all ?

JOYCE. Yes.

GERALD. It couldn't have been Babs. I was here the whole evening and nobody phoned.

C

JOYCE. Oh !... Oh, but it was Babs' voice. And she sounded ...

GERALD (*sharply*). It couldn't have been ... You dialled the wrong number, my sweet, and then you panicked. (*He rises and turns upstage.*)

JOYCE. I suppose I must have ... how silly ! Oh, I wish all this was over !

GERALD (*coming down again*). So do I. (*He sits on the arm of the settee, facing upstage*).

JOYCE. You haven't had a chance to speak to her yet ?

GERALD. About a divorce ? No.

JOYCE. You still think she'll agree ?

GERALD. I think so. Yes.

JOYCE (*rising*). Well, if not ... Gerry, I don't think it matters. (*She moves to him and puts her R. hand on his shoulder.*) I think you can divorce her. Have you heard any talk about her and Donovan ?

GERALD. Yes, I heard something this evening.

JOYCE. What ?

GERALD. Someone hinted that they might be lovers.

JOYCE. Do you think they are ?

GERALD. Possible, I suppose.

JOYCE. Do you think she can have gone away with him ?

GERALD. No. (*He rises and crosses slowly upstage to the lamp above the desk and turns it out.*)

(JOYCE *follows him across to the back of the chair* R.C.)

JOYCE. What's wrong ?

GERALD (*keeping his back to her*). Nothing.

JOYCE. Yes, there is. (*The thought suddenly strikes her.*) Gerry ! ... you wouldn't mind, would you ? You're not *fond* of her ?

GERALD. *Fond* of her !

JOYCE. Then what ?

GERALD (*turning to her*). Nothing ... nothing. It's just that I can't bring myself to talk about Babs. Not even to you. (*He takes a step towards her.*)

JOYCE. Is that all ? For a moment I thought ... Gerry, you're sure, aren't you, that it's me you love ?

GERALD (*moving closer to her*). That's the one thing in the world that I am completely sure of.

JOYCE. If ever you changed your mind, you'd tell me ? It isn't a thing one ought to find out by accident.

GERALD (*taking her hand*). But, darling, I love you. No one but you, nothing but you. I can't even start to tell you how I love you.

JOYCE. All right. (*She turns to the table behind the settee.*) Things are steadying down again now. Oh, that was dreadful !

GERALD. All right ... I know it's all a mess and a muddle, but it will come right. Joyce ... (*He takes a step towards her.*)

JOYCE. Yes. (*She turns to him.*)

GERALD. It will come right. (*He takes her hand.*)
JOYCE. Oh, why did you marry her, Gerry! You should have waited for me.
GERALD. God, I wish I had.
JOYCE. I think I ought to go now.
GERALD. Perhaps you should. I'll drive you home.

(*A bell rings somewhere in the back of the house. GERALD turns his head and stands listening.*)

JOYCE. Is it Babs?
GERALD. No.
JOYCE. Why not? It must be!
GERALD. No. She'd have come straight in, the door's not locked yet.

(*There is another loud ring, and this time the sound of knocking.*)

GERALD. I'll see who it is. (*He crosses up* L.)
JOYCE. What shall I do?
GERALD. Stay here. I won't let them in.

(GERALD *goes out up* L. JOYCE *stands motionless and listening. The door up* L. *opens quickly and* PINKIE *comes in. She is wearing a dressing gown.*)

PINKIE. That's a policeman!
JOYCE. A policeman! Are you sure?
PINKIE. Something's happened to Babs! Yes, I saw him, I saw Gerry let him in. (*She comes down to the stool* L.C.) It's Babs, I know it is. That Donovan's smashed her up.
JOYCE (*coming down* C.). Oh, no, I don't expect so. (*She comes round the* R. *end of the settee.*)
PINKIE. Well, you see. I knew there was something wrong when I didn't find her here.
JOYCE. But you said she'd gone to stay with someone.
PINKIE. No, I said she might have. And that was silly too. I knew she meant to come home to-day.
JOYCE. Pinkie, when did she leave your house? (*She sits on the settee,* R. *end.*)
PINKIE. Well, that's the point, you see. She wasn't staying with me.
JOYCE. What! Not at all?
PINKIE. No. Look here, my dear, it's a bit of a mess, and I'm wondering what I ought to say to Gerry . . . You see, she never let me know she was coming, and on the *Thursday* night she rolled up with Donovan and " Two single rooms, please, Pinkie," she said.
JOYCE. And you had no room for them?
PINKIE. Room! (*She moves to the settee and sits,* L. *end.*) I hadn't an empty bed in the house, and she might have known that, it being the night before the National.

JOYCE. So what did they do ?

PINKIE. " Well, you won't get a bed in Liverpool to-night," I said. But Bertie got on to the Adelphi for them—and by pure chance they'd just had a wire cancelling a couple of rooms.

JOYCE. So they stayed at the Adelphi, and Babs was going to say she'd been staying with you.

PINKIE. That was the idea. " Much better tell Gerry the truth," I said. " He's not the sort to go jumping to conclusions." But nothing'd persuade her. " I'm going home on Saturday," she said, " and you've got to come and stay with us. You arrive in time for dinner, and don't say anything about it and neither will I." And now, when I get here, she's not here, and all this happens.

JOYCE. Darling, nothing's happened yet. (*She rises and crosses to the fire.*)

(GERALD *comes in up* L.)

GERALD. Pinkie, I'm afraid it is Babs. (*He comes to the* L. *end of the settee and stands looking down at* PINKIE.)

PINKIE. There, what did I say !—Donovan's smashed her up !

GERALD. No, it wasn't a motor accident.

PINKIE. What was it, then ? What's happened ?

GERALD. She's dead.

(PINKIE *gives a slight moaning scream.*)

They found her in her own car in Liverpool about an hour ago. They think she was—murdered.

(JOYCE *stands like a stone. After one dazed moment,* PINKIE *bursts into tears.*)

QUICK CURTAIN.

ACT II.

SCENE.—*The same. The morning of Monday, April 6th.*
It is about mid-day. The day is warm and sunny, broken every now and then by a shower. The garden door and the window up R. *are open ; the window down* R. *is closed.*

When the CURTAIN *rises,* PINKIE *is at the 'phone and has already been talking for some time. She wears a black dress with touches of white.*

PINKIE. ... Oh, Bertie ! Did he really ? ... No, I'm sure I never told him that ... No, don't you say anything—I'll settle it when I get back ... Nonsense, Bertie ! I haven't been away as long as all that, and Gerry needed me—you know he did ...

(MORTON *enters up* L. *He holds the door for* PHILIP, *who enters. Seeing* PINKIE *at the telephone,* PHILIP *mounts the step into the alcove and waits.*)

Well, anyway, I'm leaving after lunch, I'll be home by half-past three. (*She turns and sees* MORTON *and* PHILIP.) All right, Bertie, three o'clock, then ... (*To* MORTON.) Morton, don't go away. (*Into the 'phone.*) Bertie, who d'you think's just come in ? Philip. ... Yes, all right. (*To* PHILIP.) It's Bertie. He says to give you his love.

PHILIP. Right. Love received. (*He turns upstage and selects a book from between the book-ends.*)

PINKIE (*into the 'phone*). Who ? Oh, Gerry ... no, he's not here at the moment. He's all right, dear, yes ... he's wonderful, dear ... wonderful. Well, it's over a week ago since it happened ... All right, dearie, see you this afternoon. Goo'bye. (*She ends up with three brisk little kisses, and puts down the receiver. She rises and moves above the arm-chair,* R.C.) Good morning, Philip. Morton, you needn't tell Mr. Coates that Mr. Balfour's here.

(MORTON *looks at* PHILIP.)

PHILIP. What's this, Pinkie ? I have an appointment with Gerry at twelve o'clock.

PINKIE. Yes, well you're five minutes early. Now you've got one with me at five to. I'll tell Mr. Coates in a minute, Morton. (*She crosses above the settee to* MORTON.)

(MORTON *again looks at* PHILIP.)

PHILIP. All right, Morton. (*He comes down* R. *of the settee. As he passes he drops the book on the table behind the settee.*)

MORTON. Very good, sir.

(MORTON *goes out.* PHILIP *moves round the end of the settee and sits,* R. *end.*)

PINKIE (*turning to* PHILIP). Now look, dear. I want a little talk with you I'm going home after lunch. I've been wanting a word with you ever since the inquest.

PHILIP. You always know where to find me, Pinkie.

PINKIE. Yes, but I know how busy you are. (*She comes above the* L. *end of the settee.*) Philip, why did they adjourn the inquest? What does it mean?

PHILIP. It simply means they haven't found out who did it, and they hope to know more before the resumed inquest on Friday.

PINKIE. Well, isn't it time the police got a move on? It's over a week since it happened. This local man—Gibson—he was here again last night, asking a lot of questions. " What's the use of all this? " I said. " We've told you all we know, we told you at the beginning. (*She comes down to the fireplace.*) You're all so busy asking questions," I said, " you none of you have time to think." Good heavens, I know what happened to Babs as well as if I'd been there myself!

PHILIP. Why don't you tell them then, Pinkie?

PINKIE (*moving to the* L. *arm of the settee*). Tell them! Of course I've told them! D'you think they'd listen? (*She sits on the arm.*) Look here, they *know* what happened that night. There was poor Babs in the Adelphi; she'd won a packet at Aintree, and there she was, throwing her money about, standing drinks to anyone who came into the bar. " Well," I said to Inspector Ayling, " you don't have to wonder what happened. You get me a list of who was in the bar that night," I said. " I don't say I'll tell you who did it, but I'll pick out five or six names that'll be worth looking into. You're not in the hotel business," I said, " without knowing something about the men who hang around Liverpool bars. Some of them are a lousy lot," I said, " and a good many of them'd do anything for three hundred quid."

PHILIP. Even murder?

PINKIE. Ah, but it wasn't murder. (*She rises.*) She died of heart-failure. That's one thing the doctor was clear about. (*She sits on the settee,* L. *end.*)

PHILIP. Yes, but there'd been a struggle—her injuries showed that. There's no doubt someone thought he'd killed her.

PINKIE. Oh, if only I'd let her come to me, like she wanted to! I could have found room for her somehow!

PHILIP. Pinkie, you couldn't foresee this.

PINKIE (*rising and going to the fireplace*). I ought never to have let her go off with Donovan like that, but I didn't know they were . . . I mean, I'd no idea there was anything between them. Did you know?

PHILIP (*cautiously*). I'd heard a rumour.

PINKIE. I wish I had, I'd have put a stop to it all right. Poor Babs, she never had any sense, but Donovan, of all people! It's too bad he was able to prove an alibi, I'd have liked to see him hanged.

PHILIP. Lucky for him he could prove it. I wonder where she meant to go when she left the hotel ?

PINKIE (*going up* L. *of the settee and crossing upstage to the garden door*). Oh, she meant to come back to me, I'm sure she did. She got her car out— (*She leans against the* L. *doorpost.*) —she wouldn't worry about her licence when she was in a temper—and someone followed her to the garage and asked her for a lift.

PHILIP. Someone she knew, perhaps.

PINKIE. Yes. He gets her to a quiet street, then tries to get her handbag. Remember, there's three hundred quid in that bag. Well, you wouldn't get anything away from Babs like that.

PHILIP. I must say that sounds reasonable to me.

PINKIE (*crossing upstage to* L.C.). It's reasonable to everybody except a policeman. I *know* it's what happened. And the police leave the car standing there for twenty-four hours before they open it and have a look inside ! (*She comes down to the arm-chair above the fire.*)

PHILIP. Yes, that was slow of them.

PINKIE. " You're a fine lot ! " I said to Inspector Ayling. "And if I leave my car outside a shop for five minutes, there's one of you standing by it with a notebook when I come out ! "

PHILIP. They're doing their best, no doubt. You know what Liverpool's like on National night. They'll have hard work to find anyone who noticed one particular woman, or one particular car.

PINKIE. Yes, but why don't they go on looking in Liverpool where it happened ? Not come back here asking the same old questions all over again. What Gerry needs now is a chance to forget it all. And what about the papers ? (*She moves to the settee and sits,* L. *end.*)

PHILIP. What papers ?

PINKIE. Well, the newspapers. All the muck they're dragging up about Babs and Donovan . . . photographs and headlines. Did you see the *Sunday Echo* ? Great headlines half across the page— " Shipping Magnate's Wife Found Dead in Car ! " And then all that about the shoes.

PHILIP. The *Record* made a point of that.

PINKIE. Yes, they all did, that's the sort of thing they love.

PHILIP. It does seem strange.

PINKIE. The police say the shoes must have come off in the struggle, but then why weren't they found in the car ?

PHILIP. Has Inspector Ayling been here ?

PINKIE. No, but the local man, Gibson, was here last night, asking all those questions. Look here, Philip, can't you do something about it ?

PHILIP. No, my dear, I can't. If the police have drawn blank in Liverpool, it's quite natural they should come back here.

PINKIE (*moving nearer to* PHILIP). Why ? Why here ? She left here on the Thursday and never came back, so what's the use ?

Can't you go to Headquarters and say we've told them all we know, and now they're only upsetting the servants and wasting everyone's time ?

PHILIP (*rising*).   No, Pinkie, I can't and I won't !   (*He crosses to the fireplace.*)

PINKIE.   You're Gerry's lawyer, aren't you ?   You ought to be able to keep the police out of his house.

PHILIP.   Now, Pinkie, be reasonable !   How can I stop the police acting as they think fit ?

PINKIE.   Well, I must say !   Call yourself a lawyer, and afraid to say boo to a policeman !

PHILIP.   You've a broad idea of what constitutes a boo !

(GERALD *comes in up* L.)

GERALD.   Hullo, Philip, I didn't know you were here.   (*He stands up* L.C.)

PHILIP.   Pinkie kidnapped me.

PINKIE (*rising*).   If I were you, dearie, I'd change my lawyer. (*She crosses downstage to the desk.*)   I suppose you want to see him now ?

GERALD.   Well, he has come to see me.

PINKIE.   You're welcome.   (*She picks up her handbag and crosses upstage to* GERALD.)   Would you mind if we lunch a little early ? Bertie wants me back by about three o'clock.

GERALD.   Any time you like.   Just tell Morton.

PINKIE (*continuing to the door*).   Thanks, dearie, one o'clock'll do. (*She turns at the door.*)   Better not sign anything Billy gives you till you've shown it to me.

GERALD.   Billy—— ?

PINKIE.   Ma-a-a-a-a !   (*She tugs an imaginary beard.*)

(PINKIE *goes out.*)

GERALD (*crossing to the desk*).   What have you been doing to ruffle her ?   (*He makes a brief note on the telephone pad.*)

PHILIP.   I'm not just certain.   I think she wants me to stop the police asking questions.

GERALD (*amused*).   It'd be nice if you could.

PHILIP (*going up* L. *of the settee and crossing upstage*).   Yes— they're enquiring into a good many things, Gerry.   They're asking questions about you.

GERALD.   Oh ?

PHILIP (*leaning on the back of the chair* R.C.).   That's what I've come to see you about.   I had a visit from that Detective-Inspector Ayling yesterday—he came to my office.   Have you seen him ?

GERALD (*turning to* PHILIP).   Yes, I saw him in Liverpool the day after Babs was found.   I haven't seen him since.   He seemed a very decent fellow.

PHILIP. He's a very shrewd one. I've heard him handle many a case in court.

GERALD. What did he want to see you about?

PHILIP. Well, he had a few questions to ask.

GERALD. Why did he come to you? (*He sits on the desk, upstage end, and puts his* R. *foot on the chair.*)

PHILIP. As your lawyer. For one thing, he wanted to know whether you were contemplating divorce proceedings against your wife.

GERALD. What did you say?

PHILIP. I said if you were, I'd heard nothing of it. You gave me no definite answer the other night.

GERALD. I didn't know then that I had any grounds.

PHILIP. Did Ayling ask *you* about that?

GERALD. No. He asked me if I'd known that Donovan was her lover, and I told him I hadn't. He asked what sort of terms Babs and I were on. I didn't pretend we were very affectionate, I told him we didn't get on very well together, but that I hadn't known about Donovan. In fact, I told him the truth.

PHILIP. What else did he ask you?

GERALD. Oh, he said just as a matter of form he wanted to know if I'd been in Liverpool that night. I told him I hadn't.

PHILIP. I suppose he hadn't seen our friend Darling at that time.

GERALD. Darling? I don't know. Why?

PHILIP. Well, he has seen him now, and Darling's told Ayling he thought he saw you coming back from Liverpool on the twelve forty-two that night.

(GERALD *rises and crosses downstage to the fireplace.*)

GERALD (*annoyed*). That was nice of him. (*He takes his pipe from the mantelpiece.*)

PHILIP. Oh, he meant no harm, I think. They were asking him questions, and he's a born gossip.

GERALD (*going up* L. *of the settee into the alcove.*) Did he tell them he was more than half tight at the time?

PHILIP. He didn't tell me he had. I mentioned it myself to the Inspector.

GERALD. Good for you, Philip. (*He picks up the tobacco jar.*) Anyway, it doesn't matter much, does it?

PHILIP. That's for you to say. I just thought I'd mention it.

GERALD (*filling his pipe*). What are you driving at, Philip? You're not suggesting I was in Liverpool, are you?

PHILIP (*blandly*). I'm not suggesting anything.

GERALD. Then what do you mean?

PHILIP. Well . . . I've seen so many get a bit out of their depth through an early misunderstanding with the police.

GERALD. But I've got nothing to hide from them.

PHILIP. Then that's all right, and I've wasted half a morning.

GERALD (*coming down to the table behind the settee with his pipe and the tobacco*). Why did you think I might have been in Liverpool ?

PHILIP. There are so many reasons, and some you might not care for the Inspector to know. You might have been suspicious of your wife and Donovan.

GERALD. But I wasn't, and even if I had been, I wouldn't spy on them.

PHILIP. You might have gone up with someone else, and not want that someone else pulled into a case like this.

GERALD. I see.

PHILIP. That's what it usually is, and that's why I thought I'd have a word with you. I know this man Ayling. He's all right, I think, but he's gone up pretty quickly, and he's going higher if he can. It wouldn't do to start badly with him, he's not a man to get the wrong side of if you can help it.

GERALD (*putting the tobacco jar on the table ; thoughtfully*). No, quite. (*He moves to the* L. *arm of the settee.*)

PHILIP. By the way, this isn't an official legal visit.

GERALD (*sitting on the arm, facing upstage, smilingly*). Meaning you won't charge me for it ?

PHILIP. Meaning you needn't mention it to the Inspector. (*He moves towards* GERALD.)

GERALD. I'm afraid I've been a lot of trouble to you lately, Philip.

PHILIP (*patting* GERALD'S *shoulders*). Don't be ridiculous, man ! (*He crosses above him to the door.*) So long, Gerry.

GERALD. So long.

(MORTON *enters up* L.)

MORTON. An Inspector Ayling is here, sir. He has Sergeant Gibson with him. He wants to know if he may see you for a few minutes.

GERALD. Yes, certainly. Where have you put them ?

MORTON. In the drawing-room, sir.

GERALD (*rising*). Well, show Mr. Balfour out, and then show them in here, will you ?

MORTON. Very good, sir.

GERALD. Well, good-bye, Philip. Thank you so much for coming over. I'm really very grateful to you.

PHILIP. So long, Gerry.

(PHILIP *and* MORTON *go out.* GERALD *picks up the tobacco jar and crosses to the desk. He puts the jar on the downstage* L. *corner.* MORTON *enters.*)

MORTON (*announcing*). Detective-Inspector Ayling and Sergeant Gibson.

(GERALD *crosses above the settee to up* L.C. AYLING *comes in. He is followed by* GIBSON. AYLING *is about thirty-five, good-looking and smart, wearing civilian clothes. He is clever and ambitious, but he has an easy, rather engaging surface manner.* GIBSON *is in uniform, a man of about* AYLING'S *age, but less polished. Not brilliant, but no fool, either ; and thoroughly honest and likeable.* MORTON *goes out immediately.*)

GERALD (*shaking hands*). Good morning, Inspector.
AYLING. Good morning, sir.
GERALD. 'Morning, Gibson.
GIBSON. Good morning, sir.
AYLING. I'm sorry to come down here and bother you again, sir. I know Sergeant Gibson's asked you a good many questions already.
GERALD. Oh, that's all right—Gibson and I are old friends. I think I've told him all I know about my wife's movements, but I'm afraid I wasn't much help. (*He crosses to the desk.*) Will you sit down ?
AYLING (*following* GERALD *to the chair* R.C.). Thank you, sir.
GERALD (*picking up the cigarette box and offering it*). Cigarette ?
AYLING. Thank you. (*He takes a cigarette.*)

(GIBSON *stands above the* L. *end of the settee.*)

GERALD (*offering the cigarettes*). Gibson ?
GIBSON. No thank you, sir.
GERALD (*putting the box down*). Well, how are things going ? (*He turns the desk chair to face* L.)
AYLING. Not too well, I'm afraid, sir. (*He lights his cigarette.*)
GERALD. I'm sorry to hear that. (*He sits in the desk chair.*)
AYLING (*sitting in the chair* R.C.). Well, as you know, sir, we got a bad start—the case wasn't handed over to me till the Sunday morning.
GERALD. Yes, that made things difficult for you.
AYLING. It did, sir—thirty-six hours clean wasted. We've put in a lot of work since then, but we haven't caught up. Frankly, sir, I've drawn blank in Liverpool so far, and I'm going to start again here. That's why I've come down to bother you.
GERALD (*lighting his pipe*). Here ? Well, how can I help you ?
AYLING. What I'm trying to get at now is where your wife meant to go when she left the Adelphi that Friday night. We know she quarrelled with Mr. Donovan and packed her suitcase, and then, though no one saw her do it, she must have got her car out of the garage and driven away. Now, sir, where do you think she'd make for ? (*He pauses.*)

(GERALD *considers.*)

Do you think she'd go to her sister's ?

GERALD. I think she might. That's what Mrs. Collins thinks she meant to do.

AYLING. And yet she certainly didn't get there, and Selborne Road was right out of her way.

(GIBSON *unobtrusively produces his notebook and pencil and takes notes.*)

GERALD. That's true.

AYLING. Do you think she meant to come here, sir ?

GERALD. Here ?

AYLING. Yes. To her own home.

GERALD. Oh, well—put that way—yes, I think—she may have set out to come back here.

AYLING. She might even have *come* back here.

GERALD. But she didn't.

AYLING. No-o. You don't think she could have rung, or knocked, and failed to wake anyone, and given it up and gone back to Liverpool ?

GERALD (*decidedly*). That's the last thing she'd have done. If she *had* come here, she'd have knocked and rung till somebody *did* answer. She wouldn't just turn round and go back to Liverpool on a night like that.

AYLING. No, hardly. Then can you think of any other place, about twelve miles from Liverpool, that she might have meant to go to ?

GERALD. Twelve miles ? Why twelve miles ?

AYLING. Well, sir, I have a reason for fixing that rough distance, but it isn't worth going into.

GERALD. Oh, but this is twelve miles from Liverpool.

AYLING (*as though he had only just realised it*). Yes, it is, sir. If your wife *had* come back here that night and knocked at the door —I'm sorry to appear so obstinate, sir——

GERALD. That's all right.

AYLING. If she had knocked, would you have heard her ?

GERALD. Yes, I think so. I sleep directly over the front door, and I'm a very light sleeper.

AYLING. Would the servants have heard her ?

GERALD. No, I don't think so. Oh, Morton might—he's the butler—his room's directly over mine. The other servants sleep at the back of the house, I don't think they'd hear anything.

AYLING (*to* GIBSON).   That's what you told me, Fred.

GIBSON. Yes, I'm sure Mr. Coates is right about that.

AYLING. Well, sir, I think that's about all, except, just as a matter of form—you've been very patient, sir—would you mind just running through what you did yourself that night ?

(GERALD *looks a little surprised.*)

Oh, it doesn't mean anything, sir. It's just a matter of routine that we have to follow in a case like this.

GERALD. Oh, that's all right—you can't hurt my feelings. Let's see. I dined alone about eight, as usual—I spent a very domestic evening. After dinner I read the evening paper. I listened to the wireless—heard the account of the National, wrote a letter or two, and went to bed—no, I think I switched on the wireless again and listened to something for about half an hour. Then I went to bed.

AYLING. What was it you listened to, sir ?

GERALD. Oh, really, Inspector ! Oh yes, I remember, it was a Gilbert and Sullivan programme, rather a good one.

AYLING. And you went to bed at what time, sir ?

GERALD. As soon as it was over—half-past eleven, I think.

AYLING. No one came to see you or rang you up that night ?

GERALD. I'm afraid not. If you're trying to fix an alibi for me, Inspector, I'm afraid I haven't got one.

AYLING. Oh, we needn't talk about alibis, sir ! As I say, this is just routine. You didn't go out yourself at all ?

GERALD. No.

(AYLING *rises and goes to the table behind the settee.*)

AYLING (*flicking his cigarette ash into the ashtray*). Then if Mr. Darling says he saw you on Liverpool platform after midnight that night, he's mistaken ?

GERALD. Oh, he told you that yarn, did he ?

AYLING (*turning to* GERALD). Well, sir, I've interviewed a lot of the people who saw your wife at the Adelphi that night, and he was one of them. He happened to mention that he thought he'd seen you on Liverpool platform.

GERALD. Yes, I know. He dined here the next night and said so. I told him he'd been seeing things.

AYLING (*coming above the chair* R.C.). I rather gather he might have been seeing things that night, sir.

(AYLING *and* GIBSON *exchange smiles.*)

In fact he more or less admitted it himself.

GERALD. Yes, he is quite wrong. For one thing, I always take the car into Liverpool—I haven't been up by train for at least three months—for another thing I didn't go out at all that night. No, Inspector, I've got no one to support my story, but I assure you I spent an entirely blameless evening alone here by the fire. (*He rises and moves a step upstage.*) Pity I didn't ask you up for a game of cards, Gibson.

GIBSON. Oh well, sir, we could fix that up. I could say I was here all the evening.

GERALD. That's a very handsome offer.

AYLING. Wouldn't do you much good, sir—Gibson's too well known in the Force.

GERALD. Did you two know each other before ?

AYLING. Oh, yes. We walked a beat together a long time ago.

GIBSON. I walked it, sir. He was usually in someone's warm kitchen.

AYLING. I'm glad you know him, or you might believe him. Well, thanks very much, sir, we won't take up any more of your time, but I'd just like a word with the servants, if I may.

GERALD. Oh yes, rather. I'll get hold of Morton for you. (*He crosses below the settee towards the fireplace.*)

(MORTON *enters up* L.)

(*He turns at the fireplace.*)   Oh, here he is !

MORTON (*announcing*). Miss Penrose !

(JOYCE *comes in*).

GERALD. Oh, hullo, Joyce ! Good morning. Just a minute, Morton.

JOYCE. Good morning. (*She sees the police.*) Oh, I'm sorry—I didn't know . . .

GERALD. It's all right, we've just finished. May I introduce Detective-Inspector Ayling ? Sergeant Gibson of course you know.

JOYCE. Good morning.

AYLING. Good morning, madam.

GIBSON. Good morning, madam.

(JOYCE *mounts the step into the alcove and stands* C. *with her back to the audience.*)

GERALD. Morton, Inspector Ayling would like to see the staff. Do whatever he wants you to, will you ? (*To* AYLING.) I'll be about the house if you want me, Inspector.

AYLING. Thank you, sir.

(AYLING *and* GIBSON *go out.* MORTON *follows them.*)

JOYCE (*coming down to* GERALD). Gerry—oh, Gerry, I had to come. I haven't seen you since that night. I've been thinking of you all the time—I know you must have been hating every moment of this.

GERALD. It hasn't been much fun.

JOYCE. My poor darling ! It'll die down soon, and when it's over, I'll spend the rest of my life making it up to you.

GERALD. I think you could make up to me for anything.

JOYCE. I simply couldn't stay away any longer.

GERALD. Yet all the same, my sweet, you must. You mustn't come here. Whatever happens, you mustn't be involved in this.

JOYCE (*breaking* R.). Oh, Gerry, no one's thinking about me. Haven't the police got anything yet ? (*She drops her bag on the settee.*)

GERALD. Well, they've got an idea now that Babs came back here that night.

JOYCE. That Friday night ? I think so, too.

GERALD (*turning to face the fire*). It's damn silly. She couldn't have.

JOYCE. But couldn't she ? Are you sure ? I told you I rang up that night, and I thought she answered. That's partly why I came over. Gerry—do you think I ought to tell the police ?

GERALD. No. (*He puts his pipe on the mantelpiece.*)

JOYCE. Why not ? I could say I rang up wanting to speak to her—about bridge or something.

GERALD. And rang off the moment she answered ? (*He turns to her.*)

JOYCE. Yes, that's true. Well, why don't I tell them the truth ?

(GERALD *crosses downstage to* c.)

Does it matter now ? I mean, this is serious.

GERALD. Have you told anyone ?

JOYCE. No, of course I haven't.

GERALD. Then don't.

JOYCE. Gerry, I don't understand. Is there some reason—something I don't know about ?

GERALD (*having made up his mind ; going briskly up to the garden door*). Yes. (*He closes the door.*)

JOYCE. Well—what is it ? (*She crosses below the settee and goes up to the chair* R.C.)

GERALD (*coming* R. *of the chair* R.C.). She did come back.

JOYCE. She did ! And you've told them she didn't.

GERALD. She did come back. And I killed her.

JOYCE. Gerry ! (*She drops into the chair and turns to face him.*) It isn't true !

GERALD. It is. I wish to God it wasn't, but it is.

JOYCE. Do you mean you murdered her ?

GERALD. No. It was an accident.

JOYCE (*after a pause*). Tell me.

GERALD. She came back late that Friday night. She'd been drinking a lot. I tried to persuade her to go to bed but she wouldn't, and we had a row. She behaved like a madwoman. She went for me with that paper-knife. She fought like a demon, I think she was mad. I managed to get hold of her somehow, and I hit her, hit her hard—I had to. She fell with her head against the corner of that desk. When I picked her up, she was dead.

JOYCE (*rising*). But a doctor—didn't you send for a doctor ?

GERALD. She was dead.

JOYCE. The police, then ! Gerry, why didn't you ? Oh, my God, why didn't you ! It was an accident !

GERALD. D'you think they'd have believed that ? I had no witness that she went for me, and if they'd wanted to call it murder, they hadn't to look far for a motive.

JOYCE. You mean me ?
GERALD. Yes.
JOYCE. I see.
GERALD. Or as it happened, they might have thought I'd found out about Donovan. (*He turns away* R.) Either of those would do.
JOYCE. But, Gerry, she died of heart-failure !
GERALD (*looking out of the window*). I didn't know that then, I thought I'd killed her. I *had* killed her.
JOYCE. But they wouldn't have called it murder !
GERALD. No—manslaughter. They wouldn't have hanged me, they'd have sent me to prison. I'd rather be hanged.

(*There's a moment's silence.*)

JOYCE. I still don't understand. She was found in Liverpool.
GERALD (*turning to her*). I drove her back in her own car.
JOYCE (*horrified*). *You drove her back*—Oh, my God !
GERALD (*taking a step towards her*). Listen Joyce——
JOYCE (*backing to the up* R. *corner of the settee and sitting against it*). No, Gerry, no ! (*She controls herself with an effort.*) I'm sorry.
GERALD. I know how you must be feeling. I'd have given anything not to have had to tell you.
JOYCE. I still don't quite believe it . . . Oh, Gerry, I'm so frightened for you.
GERALD (*moving to her*). Darling, you needn't be. (*He takes her hand.*) It'll be all right.
JOYCE. A few moments ago I was thinking soon all this would would be over and then we could get married.
GERALD. And now ?
JOYCE. Now knowing about it—being terrified for the rest of our lives. Oh, Gerry (*she rises*) why didn't you tell them ? You must have been mad ! (*She crosses below the settee to the fire.*)
GERALD. No, I was quite sane, and even now I'd do the same again. You haven't thought it out, you don't realize what it would have meant. Arrested, tried, and sent to prison. However short a sentence they'd given me, I was done for. I'd lost everything— I'd lost you.
JOYCE (*turning to him*). No, you wouldn't have lost me.
GERALD. D'you think I'd have asked you to wait while I served my sentence ?
JOYCE. But of course I would have waited. (*She turns to the fire and leans on the mantelpiece.*)
GERALD. No, once out of prison, you'd never have seen me again.

(JOYCE *turns to him.*)

JOYCE. Gerry . . . all this was on the Friday night ?
GERALD. Yes.
JOYCE. . . . And on the Saturday night I dined here.
GERALD. Yes.
JOYCE. And Philip, and Buns, and Pinkie ?

GERALD. Yes. Yes, and I laughed and talked and played bridge. That's what you're thinking, isn't it ?

JOYCE. Yes.

GERALD. And you stayed behind after the others had gone—d'you remember ?

JOYCE. Yes.

GERALD. And we talked, and I told you how much I loved you, and now you're shocked—you're wondering how I could have done it. But don't you see I had to ? You expected me to, didn't you ?

JOYCE. I suppose I did.

GERALD. You'd have thought it queer if I hadn't, wouldn't you ?

JOYCE. I suppose I would . . . were you expecting Buns that night ?

GERALD. Yes.

JOYCE. And Pinkie too ?

GERALD. Yes, Babs had told me they'd both be there. You were the one I didn't expect.

JOYCE (*moving* R. *a step*). I tried to talk about Babs divorcing you, and you wouldn't. I've wondered about it once or twice.

GERALD. Yes. That was a bad mistake, I mustn't make another.

JOYCE. Don't talk like that ! (*She crosses to the* R. *end of the settee.*) Gerry, please !

GERALD. What ?

JOYCE. Please ! Tell them !—tell them now !

GERALD. Tell the police ? No.

JOYCE. It was an accident. They'll know that now—they know she died of heart-failure . . .

GERALD. It's still manslaughter. I won't do it, Joyce—I won't chuck my hand in just because it's hard to play.

JOYCE (*kneeling on the settee,* R. *end and facing* GERALD *across the back*). Gerry, it's the only way ! Whatever happens, however long it is, I'll wait for you.

GERALD. No. Listen, Joyce, I've never talked about Babs to anyone, not even to you. No one knows what it was like to live with her. For ten years she tried her hardest to make my life a hell, and, my God, she succeeded ! I didn't mean to kill her—I'd have given anything if she'd been alive, but she was dead, and I felt I owed her very little. (*He crosses below the settee to* R. *of the arm-chair above the fire.*) I swore that night that I wouldn't let her ruin my life and yours, and I'm not going to . . . I didn't mean to kill her. Don't you believe that ?

JOYCE. Yes, I *know* you didn't mean to.

GERALD (*coming down to* L. *of the stool* L.C.). Then I've committed no crime. Why do you want me to give myself up ? (*He goes up again to* R. *of the arm-chair above the fire.*)

JOYCE. Because you haven't a chance. Once they think she came back here, they'll start looking round, and in the end they'll

D

find something.

GERALD (*coming down a step*). But, darling, there's nothing to find.

JOYCE. But the servants——

GERALD (*coming down to the stool*). They'd all gone to bed. (*He sits on the stool.*)

JOYCE. Gerry ! She *did* speak to me that night on the telephone ! Didn't she ?

GERALD. I think she must have. She left her suit-case in the car, and I went to fetch it. It must have happened then.

JOYCE. Gerry ! That's what I mean—that's how they'll get you ! Something you didn't know about ! Something you've never even thought of. Anyone may have seen you—seen you in Liverpool. Did you come back from Liverpool that night by train ?

GERALD. Yes.

JOYCE. Then someone did see you ! Buns ! He said so. *Did* he see you ?

GERALD. Yes.

JOYCE. Suppose he tells the police ?

GERALD. He has told them.

JOYCE. Gerry !

GERALD. It's all right—he was drunk. His evidence isn't worth a damn. I've told them a perfectly plausible story, and I'm going to stick to it. (*He rises and moves to the fireplace.*)

JOYCE (*rising*). How can you be so confident ?

GERALD (*soberly*). I am pretty confident. I knew it was a risk— a big risk—but I weighed up the chances that night, and I thought they were worth taking. The worst chance I took was driving the car back in the fog. I had to hurry, and if I'd hit anything, I was done. Well, I didn't—I got there. And now over a week's gone by, and every day makes me safer. If they don't find out very soon, they never will.

JOYCE. Yes, Gerry ; but at any moment—oh, my God, I can't bear it ! (*She sits on the settee, R. end.*)

GERALD (*going to the settee and sitting, L. end*). Joyce, don't torture yourself by going through it all—it's no use. I've thought of all this. I've thought of nothing else for nine days, and you won't think of anything fresh. Try to put it out of your head— try to forget you know. Make yourself believe you don't . . . (*He hears* MORTON *outside the room and breaks off.*)

JOYCE. Gerry, I can't. (*She rises and crosses to the desk.*)

(MORTON *enters up* L.)

MORTON. Excuse me, sir. Inspector Ayling wants to know if he may have a word with you.

GERALD. What, again ? Where is he ?

MORTON. In the dining room, sir. He's been interviewing the maids.

GERALD. And he wants to see me now ?

MORTON. Yes, sir. I may be wrong, sir, but I fancy it's about something Hoskyns has told him.

GERALD. All right. Tell him I'll see him in two minutes, and when you've done that, come back here.

MORTON. Very good, sir.

(MORTON *exits up* L.)

JOYCE (*crossing to* R. *of the settee*). Who's Hoskyns ?

GERALD. The housemaid.

JOYCE. Gerry, they've found out something !

GERALD (*rising and going to the arm-chair above the fire*). No, they haven't—they can't have done.

JOYCE (*crossing below the settee to him*). They have ! Oh, why won't you tell them. Gerry, this is madness !

GERALD. Joyce, you must leave this to me—you won't make me change my mind. You must go now.

JOYCE. Gerry——

GERALD. No, you haven't had time to think—I have. Go home, and don't worry, it's going to be all right. And try to see it my way—try Joyce.

(MORTON *enters up* L.)

JOYCE (*turning to the settee and picking up her bag*). All right, I'll try. (*She crosses upstage to the garden door.*) Good-bye, Gerry. When shall I see you again ? (*She stands in the doorway, her back to the* R. *doorpost.*)

GERALD (*following her*). Very soon, now. (*He stands against the* L. *doorpost.*) I'll ring you. And try, Joyce !

JOYCE. Yes, all right, I'll try.

(JOYCE *goes out through the garden door and off* L. GERALD *closes the door.*)

GERALD (*going to the table behind the settee*). Has the Inspector finished with you, Morton ?

MORTON (*coming above the* L. *end of the settee*). I haven't seen the Inspector yet, sir. I told him I had nothing to add to what I told Sergeant Gibson last night.

GERALD. Is he upsetting the maids much ?

MORTON. It's Hoskyns, sir.

GERALD. What's the matter with Hoskyns ?

MORTON. Well, sir, she's been behaving very oddly since Sergeant Gibson was here last night. This morning she informed me that she was in possession of a valuable clue, as she called it, that she would only communicate to the police.

GERALD. Clue ? What sort of clue ?

MORTON. I don't know, sir. That was all she would tell me.

GERALD. You know the police have a theory now that Mrs.

Coates came back here that night ?

MORTON. So I gather, but to me it seems impossible. Had Mrs. Coates returned, sir, you or I could hardly have failed to hear the car.

GERALD. That's what I told the Inspector. You heard nothing unusual that night, did you ?

MORTON. Nothing, sir.

GERALD. Does Hoskyns think she did ?

MORTON. I don't think so, sir. I gather her " clue " is—well—something more tangible, as you might say. I'm afraid she's a very silly girl, sir.

GERALD. I'm afraid she is. Oh, well, she's young, she'll probably grow out of it.

(PINKIE *comes in up* L. *She is wearing a man's mackintosh, and she has a basket.*)

PINKIE. Gerry, we're never going to get any lunch. It's nearly a quarter to one now, and the police are still in the dining-room, interviewing the servants.

MORTON. Excuse me, madam, lunch will be ready at one. The police have finished with Mrs. Sykes, and I'll ask them to leave the dining-room now.

PINKIE. Well I'm sure they will if you tell them to, Morton. (*She puts the basket in the alcove.*)

GERALD. All right, Morton. Tell the Inspector I'll see him now.

MORTON. Very good, sir.

(MORTON *goes out up* L.)

PINKIE (*coming down to the fireplace*). I borrowed your mac., dearie. You don't mind, do you ? It was just beginning to rain.

GERALD. Not at all—it's very becoming. (*He sits on the back of the settee,* R. *end, facing upstage.*)

PINKIE. What *are* the police doing, Gerry ?

GERALD. Well, they've got an idea now that Babs came back here that night.

PINKIE. What night ? The night she died ? How could she possibly have, without your knowing ?

GERALD (*turning to* PINKIE). Well, I understand that Hoskyns has provided them with a " CLUE," in capital letters.

PINKIE. Hoskyns ? The housemaid ? What nonsense ! Can I stay ?

GERALD. Yes, do. If he doesn't want you, he can say so.

PINKIE (*taking off the mackintosh and putting it on the arm-chair above the fire*). I told you what would happen, dearie. (*She sits on the settee,* R. *end.*) Are they allowed to upset the whole house like this ?

GERALD (*rising*). Yes, of course they are, Pinkie. And don't you be cross with them. They're doing their best, and they're very decent fellows.

(*There is a knock at the door.*)

Come in.

(AYLING *enters up* L. *He closes the door.* GERALD *crosses up* L.C. *to meet him.*)

Oh, come in, Inspector. I hear you want to see me.

AYLING. Just for a minute, sir.

GERALD. Is it private, or can Mrs. Collins stay ?

(AYLING *hesitates a moment.*)

AYLING (*moving to* GERALD *above the* L. *end of the settee*). I'd be glad if she'd stay, she might be able to help us. (*He takes a mirror out of his pocket and slips it out of its case.*) Have you ever seen this before, sir ? (*He hands the mirror to* GERALD.)

GERALD (*examining it*). Not that I know of.

AYLING (*taking the mirror back*). Have you, madam ? (*He comes down to the* L. *end of the settee and exhibits it to* PINKIE.)

PINKIE. I've seen lots like it. It's an ordinary pocket mirror out of a woman's handbag.

AYLING. Not so very ordinary, madam. (*To* GERALD.) When we found Mrs. Coates, sir, her bag was in the car—rather a large, brown bag with a yellow lining. There's a pocket in it, obviously meant to hold a mirror, but the mirror is missing.

GERALD. And you think this is it ?

AYLING. Well, you can see, sir. It's backed with yellow. I'll have to find if it fits the bag, but I'm pretty sure it will.

PINKIE. Where was it found ?

AYLING. In this room, madam.

PINKIE. By the housemaid ?

AYLING. Yes.

GERALD. When did she find it ?

AYLING. On the Saturday morning, sir—the morning after Mrs. Coates was killed.

PINKIE. Then Mrs. Coates must have left it behind on the Thursday.

AYLING. Possibly, madam, but the housemaid is quite certain it was not here on the Friday.

GERALD. Where exactly did she find it ?

AYLING. Down the side of one of these arm-chairs, sir. (*He looks round.*) That one, I believe. (*He points to the arm-chair below the fire.*)

(GERALD *sits on the* L. *arm of the settee.*)

PINKIE. Then it might have been there for weeks !

AYLING. Not quite weeks, Mrs. Collins. That bag was new. Mrs. Coates only bought it the day before she went away.

(*There is a knock at the door up* L.)

GERALD. Come in.

(SERGEANT GIBSON *comes in. He has a small, brown paper parcel in his hand. He closes the door behind him.*)

AYLING (*going up* L. *to* GIBSON). Yes, Gibson ?

GIBSON. Nothing, sir. If I may have a word with you in a moment. (*He stands with his back to the door.*)

AYLING. All right. (*He comes down* L. *of the settee. To* PINKIE ; *more persuasively.*) Now, Mrs. Collins, I wonder if you can help us about this mirror. Mrs. Coates was in your house for a time on the Thursday evening, wasn't she ? (*He sits on the stool* L.C. *facing* PINKIE.)

PINKIE. Yes, for about half an hour.

AYLING. And I expect you saw her at Aintree next day ?

PINKIE. Yes, once or twice.

AYLING. Then you probably saw her make up her face, or powder her nose. I mean, ladies do it all the time, don't they ?

PINKIE. No, Inspector—they don't do anything all the time.

AYLING. In her bag, your sister had a small, round flap-jack, I think it's called—about so big. (*He makes a round with the forefingers and thumbs of his two hands.*) Now, can you remember whether she used a mirror at any time ? I mean, can you think back, and try to get a mental picture ?

PINKIE (*thinking hard*). Er . . . Yes !

(GERALD *rises. He finds himself face to face with* GIBSON *and comes down to the fireplace.*)

AYLING. You can ?

PINKIE. On Friday, at Aintree—yes, she had a mirror.

AYLING. A little mirror in a flapjack or this one.

(GERALD *takes out his cigarette case.*)

PINKIE (*slowly*). It was pouring with rain, and she opened—no, she handed me her umbrella and said, " Hold this, Pinkie." Then she opened her bag and took out a mirror . . . (*She pauses.*) It had . . . it . . .

(GERALD *opens his cigarette case and takes a cigarette.*)

GERALD (*moving to* AYLING *and leaning over his shoulder offering his case*). Cigarette ?

AYLING (*shortly*). No thank you, sir. Well, Mrs. Collins ?

PINKIE. Damn, I can't remember what it was like.

AYLING (*rising and going up* L. *of the settee*). That's a pity, madam.

(GERALD *turns to the fireplace and lights his cigarette.*)

PINKIE. It's nearly a fortnight ago, Inspector, and anyway, I don't know what it's all about.

AYLING (*coming down again to the stool* L.C.). I'm trying to trace your sister's movements on the Friday night, madam. This mirror was found in this room on the Saturday morning. If you had remembered your sister having it with her at Aintree on Friday, or if I can find anyone else who remembers it, it would be hard to see how it got back here. (*To* GERALD.) Unless, sir, your wife *was* in this room on Friday night.

GERALD. Yes, that's fairly obvious.

PINKIE. Then the answer is she *didn't* have it with her—it must have been here all the time. (*To* AYLING.) No, don't tell me Hoskyns says it wasn't here. From what I've seen of that girl's work—(*to* GERALD) I'm sorry to be rude about your servants, duckie.

GERALD. That's all right.

PINKIE. From what I've seen, she'd miss something bigger than a mirror. She left my breakfast tray in my room all yesterday and said she hadn't noticed it.

GERALD. There's one thing I don't quite understand, Inspector. Why didn't she mention this until this morning ?

AYLING. When she found the mirror on the Saturday morning, sir, no one knew that any harm had come to Mrs. Coates. After that, it passed out of her mind.

PINKIE. That girl hasn't got a mind.

GERALD. Well, I'm afraid we haven't helped you much. Is that all ?

AYLING. That's all, sir. I'd just like to ask your butler about this. I'll see him in the dining-room, if I may. (*He goes up* L. *of the settee.*)

GIBSON. Excuse me, sir, we've been turned out of the dining-room.

(AYLING *drops back above the* L. *end of the settee.*)

GERALD. I'm afraid that's Morton—Mrs. Collins wants lunch at one. (*He goes to the door up* L.) I'll send him in here.

GIBSON. May I have just a word with the Inspector first, sir ?

GERALD (*good humouredly*). Yes, I'll leave you this room. Do just what you like with the whole house. Ring for my butler when you want him.

(AYLING *crosses to the stool up* R. *He picks up the magazine and looks at it.*)

GIBSON. Thank you, sir. (*He comes into the room.*)

GERALD (*opening the door*). Are you coming, Pinkie ?

PINKIE (*rising and moving to the arm-chair above the fire*). Yes, dear, we want some more daffodils. (*She picks up the mackintosh.*)

GIBSON. Allow me, madam. (*He helps her into it.*)

PINKIE. I must look a sight in this. It's Mr. Coates', really.

GIBSON. It'll keep you dry, madam, and that's the main thing.

PINKIE. Yes, of course it is, or anyway it ought to be, at my age.

(GIBSON *hands her the basket.*)

Thank you. (*She crosses him and goes to the garden door.*) I'm sure the Inspector doesn't want my advice, but if I were you, I'd tell him not to pay too much attention to that housemaid.

GIBSON (*smiling and glancing at* AYLING). I'll tell the Inspector what you say, madam.

(PINKIE *goes out through the garden door and off* L.)

GERALD (*to* AYLING). Can I send you in a drink ? Beer, whisky or sherry or anything ?

AYLING. No, thank you, sir, I very rarely drink in the morning.

GERALD. What about you, Gibson ?

GIBSON. No, thank you sir, I couldn't after that !

GERALD. I didn't know you were shy !

(GERALD *goes out up* L.)

GIBSON (*putting his parcel on the table behind the settee*). Any good ?

AYLING (*coming down to the desk*). No. (*He picks up the telephone pad and glances at it.*)

GIBSON. Neither of them recognised it ?

AYLING. No. (*He puts down the pad.*) I didn't expect they would. (*He crosses downstage to* C.) Ring through to Liverpool when we finish here this morning, and get the bag sent down. (*He moves above the stool* L.C.) I'll bet you five pounds the mirror fits it. (*He looks at* BAB'S *picture over the fireplace.*)

GIBSON. Oh, I'm not saying it doesn't ; I'm only saying it doesn't get you much further if it does.

AYLING (*moving up* L. *of the settee*). That's as may be. (*He sees* GIBSON'S *parcel and stops by the* L. *end of the settee.*) What've you got there ?

GIBSON (*unwrapping the parcel*). One pair lady's brown walking shoes—property of the late Mrs. Coates.

AYLING. Well ?

GIBSON. Your friend the housemaid found them in a cupboard in the butler's pantry. Noticed them first on the Saturday morning —she's sure they weren't there on the Friday. And she *thinks* Mrs. Coates took them to Liverpool with her.

(AYLING *whistles.*)

GIBSON. I thought that'd please you.

AYLING. Does this butler fellow know you've got them ?

GIBSON. Well, I didn't tell him, and I don't imagine the girl has.

AYLING. All right, let's have him in. (*He breaks upstage.*)

GIBSON. O.K. (*He comes down* L. *of the settee to the fireplace.*)

AYLING (*crossing upstage to the desk*). What sort of a chap is he ? I've hardly seen him. (*He looks at the 'phone pad.*)

GIBSON. Oh, faithful retainer—a bit old and doddery ; pig-headed, sure of himself. What he says he'll stick to, and you won't shake him. Excuse me, old man, I'll just ring for my butler. (*He rings the bell.*)

AYLING. Ringing for the barmaid in the local's as far as you'll ever get.

GIBSON (*going up* L. *of the table behind the settee*). I don't have to ring for 'em, Bert—they line up when I come in. (*He wraps up the shoes.*)

AYLING. Must be the uniform. (*He crosses to the* R. *end of the table behind the settee.*) Did you ask this fellow anything about Coates ?—rows with his wife, and that sort of thing ?

(MORTON *opens the door up* L.)

GIBSON. Coates ! But, Bert . . .

(AYLING *sees* MORTON, *and stops* GIBSON *with a gesture.* MORTON *enters.*)

AYLING. Come in, Mr. Morton. I'm sorry to bother you, but I won't keep you long. (*He moves down to the table* R. *of the settee.*)

MORTON. I have to serve luncheon in ten minutes, Inspector.

AYLING. Five'll be plenty for me. Please sit down.

MORTON (*coming down* R. *of the chair above the fireplace*). I'll stand, thank you.

AYLING. I'm afraid I've rather upset your staff.

MORTON. It doesn't take much to upset some of them.

AYLING (*crossing to the fireplace*). I didn't ask them much, of course, I saved the more important questions for you.

MORTON. I answered all Sergeant Gibson's questions last night, Inspector.

AYLING (*turning below the chair above the fireplace*). Yes, I know, but there are one or two points he didn't touch on. Tell me—you've got a very nice place here, haven't you ? I should think you're very lucky with Mr. Coates ?

MORTON. I am, extremely lucky.

AYLING. A very nice gentleman, indeed, I should think. Mrs. Coates, now—— (*He pauses.*)

(MORTON *does not help.*)

I gather there was a good bit of talk locally about Mrs. Coates.

MORTON. I am not in the habit of gossiping with the local people about my employers, Inspector.

AYLING. Of course not—I'm sure you wouldn't dream of it—but you realise now, Mr. Morton, that a crime has been committed. Certain questions have to be asked, and I have to have the answers.

MORTON (*after a pause*). Mrs. Coates was not very well liked locally.

AYLING. Hit the bottle a bit, didn't she ?

MORTON. Mrs. Coates did indulge rather freely, Inspector.

AYLING. Was there any trouble about that ?

MORTON. Trouble ? In what way, Inspector ?

AYLING. Well, I mean rows—scenes between her and Mr. Coates ?

MORTON. Mr. Coates is not the sort of gentleman to make scenes, especially in front of the staff.

AYLING. And you never overheard anything ? No rows ?

MORTON. Never.

AYLING. Not even on the Friday night ?

MORTON. The—oh, which Friday ?

AYLING. The night of the Grand National.

MORTON. Mrs. Coates was not here on that night. I have already told Sergeant Gibson that.

AYLING. Oh, yes. And, talking of that night . . . you heard Mr. Coates go up to bed ?

MORTON. Yes.

AYLING. About what time ?

MORTON. About half-past eleven.

AYLING. If he'd got up again, would you have heard him ?

MORTON. Yes, I think so.

AYLING. And you didn't hear him ?

MORTON. No.

AYLING. You're quite certain you heard nothing unusual that night—no car drive up to the house ?

MORTON. No, nothing.

AYLING. I expect this must have been a great shock to Mr. Coates.

MORTON. Naturally.

AYLING. But of course he's quite young, he'll get over it. He'll be marrying again before long, I expect.

MORTON. Mrs. Coates was only buried last week, Inspector.

AYLING (*pointedly*). Some husbands start thinking of that sort of thing even before their wives are buried.

(MORTON *ignores this.*)

Oh, I'm sure Mr. Coates isn't that sort, but was there any lady who came to the house a good bit—especially, perhaps, when Mrs. Coates was away ?

MORTON. No.

AYLING. So if local gossip couples Mr. Coates' name with anyone else's—say, Miss Penrose's—that's quite a mistake ?

MORTON. Quite, I should think, Inspector.

AYLING. Does Miss Penrose come here much ?

MORTON. Miss Penrose is a fairly frequent visitor, but not unduly so. May I remind you, Inspector, that Miss Penrose's father is a son of the Earl of Cottleigh ?

AYLING (*crossing below the settee to* C.). If you were a policeman, Mr. Morton, you wouldn't trust even an earl, far less his grand-daughter. (*He turns.*) Now, just one question or two, perhaps.

(*He crosses to the stool,* L.C.) This mirror—have you ever seen it before ? (*He takes the mirror from his pocket and shows it to* MORTON.)

MORTON (*coming down a step*). No.

AYLING. Just before Mrs. Coates went away, she bought a new bag. You didn't hear her speak of having lost the mirror out of it ?

MORTON. No. Where was this found, Inspector ?

AYLING. I'm asking questions now, Mr. Morton. You've never seen it before ?

MORTON. No.

(AYLING *returns the mirror to his pocket.*)

AYLING. Have you got that parcel, Gibson ?

GIBSON. Here, sir. (*He hands the shoes, without their wrapping, to* AYLING.)

AYLING (*to* MORTON). You can hardly say you haven't seen these shoes before. (*He holds them out.*)

(*There is a short pause.*)

Well ?

MORTON. They're Mrs. Coates'—aren't they ?

AYLING. I'm asking you. (*He gives* MORTON *the shoes.*)

MORTON (*taking them and looking at them*). Yes, I think they're Mrs. Coates'.

AYLING. Do you know where they were found ?

MORTON. In the cupboard in my pantry ?

AYLING. Yes.

MORTON. Then they are Mrs. Coates'—or they were. Tck, tck, tck ! I had forgotten all about them.

AYLING. Forgotten them, had you ? What were they doing in your cupboard ?

MORTON. Oh, Mrs. Coates gave them to me.

AYLING. To have them repaired ? They're almost new. (*He takes the shoes back.*)

MORTON. Oh, no—Mrs. Coates complained they were uncomfortable. She said I might dispose of them.

AYLING. Funny she should give them to you, wasn't it ? Why not to one of the maids ?

MORTON. I was passing her bedroom door at the time, and she called, "Hoskyns ?" I said, "No, madam, this is Morton." She called me in and gave me the shoes.

AYLING. What did she say exactly ?

MORTON. I think she said, "Here, get rid of these, they give me hell."

(AYLING *turns and gives the shoes to* GIBSON. GIBSON *puts them on the table again.*)

AYLING. When was this ?

MORTON. Over a fortnight ago.

AYLING. A fortnight? Are you prepared to swear to that in court?

MORTON. Certainly, Inspector. If anyone is interested in a pair of old shoes.

AYLING. They might be. So these shoes have been in your cupboard for a fortnight?

MORTON. Yes.

AYLING. And if that girl Hoskyns says they didn't appear there until the day after the National, she's not telling the truth?

MORTON. She certainly is not.

(AYLING *turns away and crosses to the table* R. *of the settee.*)

AYLING. That'll be all, Mr. Morton. I'm sorry to have interrupted your work. (*He turns to* MORTON.) Would you ask Mr. Coates if he can spare me just two minutes?

MORTON. Very good. (*He moves up* L. *towards the door. He glances at the clock, and adds gently.*) Mr. Coates is lunching at one, Inspector.

(MORTON *goes out up* L. AYLING *moves to the chair* R.C. *and sits up* L.)

GIBSON (*moving down* L. *of the settee to the fireplace*). He put you in your place once or twice.

AYLING. Bloody old snob. Do you think he was telling the truth about those shoes?

GIBSON. Yes.

AYLING. I don't know. Is that girl prepared to swear they weren't in the cupboard before the Saturday?

GIBSON. Not she! She swore they weren't, but then she said she wouldn't swear to it.

AYLING (*exasperated*). Damn it! Can't *one* of these servants remember what shoes the woman went to Liverpool in?

GIBSON. The parlourmaid's sure they were brown.

(AYLING *looks up, interested.*)

We found eight pairs of brown.

AYLING. Oh! . . . (*He rises and moves to the desk.*)

GIBSON. Can't see any point in those shoes, Bert. Why take off her shoes and put them where they're likely to be found?

AYLING. She might have been giving a bit of trouble. Don't you take a drunk's boots off before you put him in the cells? (*He crosses above the settee.*)

GIBSON. Yes, but if I murdered him and moved the corpse, I'd put 'em on again. I wouldn't leave 'em in the cell.

AYLING. You might be a bit rattled . . . (*He turns and crosses down* R.) Of course, the old fool's heard them having rows! All the others have, and Coates didn't bother to deny it. (*He pauses a moment.*) I thought Coates was almost too confiding about that.

GIBSON (*taking a step forward*). Coates? My God, Bert, don't tell me you're hoping to put Coates in the dock?

AYLING (*slowly*). Coates had a pretty good motive—Donovan.

GIBSON. Any husband's got a motive for murdering his wife about once a week. (*He turns back to the fireplace.*) I could have murdered my old woman a dozen times. Coates isn't a murderer any more than I am.

AYLING. I don't say he is. The trouble with you, Fred, is that you like him and you didn't like her.

GIBSON. That wouldn't help him if I thought he'd committed a murder.

AYLING (*crossing to the stool* L.C. *and facing* GIBSON.) You can't get it into your head that this wasn't a deliberate murder. Someone had a row with the woman. He handled her a bit rough, and when he found she was dead, he didn't feel like telling us. That might fit Coates.

GIBSON. Well, yes, it might.

AYLING. But if she did come back to this house, it's pretty certain Coates would have known it. You'll admit that ?

GIBSON. Yes.

AYLING. So, *if* we can prove she came back here, or *if* we can prove Coates was in Liverpool when he says he wasn't, it's odds on he's our man.

GIBSON. Give you the first bit. If he's lying about her coming back here, you're probably right, but I don't think he was in Liverpool. I watched him this morning, and I reckon he was telling a straight story.

AYLING. You're forgetting one thing. Darling saw him on Liverpool platform that night.

GIBSON. You're forgetting two.

AYLING. What ?

GIBSON. First, Morton says Coates was in bed. Second, Darling admits he was bottled. Anyway, drunk or sober, put Darling up against Morton in the witness box and Darling's a hundred to eight and no takers.

AYLING (*turning away and crossing below the settee to* R.C.). I know ! *And* Coates rode the winner of your ruddy race, *and* he comes from your precious one-horse village, so he couldn't possibly do anything wrong !

GIBSON. No need to be rude about it.

AYLING (*turning back to* C.). My God, Fred, you may be pretty quick on to it when somebody robs a chicken roost . . .

GIBSON. I said there was no need to be rude. I judge a man by what I know about him, and I know Coates is straight.

(GERALD *comes in from off* L. *by the garden door.*)

GERALD. Sorry to keep you, Inspector, I was in the garden. Anything fresh ? (*He comes down to the desk.*)

AYLING (*going up* C. *to the* L. *of the table behind the settee*). Yes, sir—these. These shoes. (*He picks up the shoes and turns to* GERALD, *holding them out.*)

(GERALD *crosses to* AYLING *and takes the shoes. He turns downstage to the* R. *end of the table behind the settee and stands looking at them in silence for a moment.*)

GERALD. Whose are they ?
AYLING. Your wife's, I think, sir.
GERALD. Well ?
AYLING. You heard at the inquest that when your wife was found she had no shoes on, and they weren't in the car.
GERALD. Yes, I heard that. Where were these found ?
AYLING. In your butler's pantry, sir.
GERALD. In Morton's pantry ?
AYLING. Yes, sir.
GERALD. What does he say about them ?
AYLING. He says Mrs. Coates gave them to him a fortnight ago. She said they were too tight for her.

(GERALD *hands back the shoes.*)

GERALD (*breaking* R.). Oh, well ! Then this can't be the missing pair.
AYLING. You've no idea what shoes your wife took to Liverpool, I suppose ? (*He puts the shoes back on the table.*)
GERALD. Not the slightest, but Mrs. Collins might know. (*He goes up to the garden door and calls.*) Pinkie !
PINKIE. Oo-oo !
GERALD. Just a minute.
PINKIE (*off*). Coming.

(GERALD *comes down to the desk.*)

AYLING (*following* GERALD *to* R.C.). You think it's likely, sir, that Mrs. Coates would have given a pair of her shoes to the butler and not to one of the maids ?
GERALD. Quite likely, I think, and if Morton says so, I'm quite sure she did.
AYLING. He'd have no motive for concealing the truth, I suppose ?
GERALD (*very much surprised*). Morton ? Good heavens, no !

(PINKIE *enters, from off* L., *by the garden door. She carries a basket of daffodils.*)

PINKIE (*crossing up* C. *into the alcove*). Lunch ready ? (*She puts the basket down in the alcove up* C.)

(AYLING *turns and follows her up to the table above the settee.*)

GERALD. No, the Inspector wants to ask you something.
AYLING. I'm sorry to bother you, madam—one last question.

Can you tell me what shoes your sister was wearing at Aintree ?

PINKIE (*coming down from the alcove to* L. *of* AYLING). What shoes ? Yes, I can, as a matter of fact. She wasn't wearing shoes at all, she was wearing little short boots.

AYLING. Yes, we found those in her suit-case. Can you say what she was wearing when she came to your house on the Thursday ?

(PINKIE *thinks for a moment.*)

PINKIE. No, I'm sorry, I can't.

AYLING (*picking up the shoes and showing them to her*). Do you recognise this pair ?

PINKIE. Well, they're about her size, and the sort of shoes she wore. Oh ! Are those the missing shoes ? Where did you find them ?

AYLING. In the butler's pantry, madam.

PINKIE. In Morton's pantry !

AYLING. Yes.

PINKIE. You said they were the missing shoes !

AYLING. No, madam, excuse me, I did not.

PINKIE (*moving down* L. *of the settee, patting all her pockets*). Where's my handkerchief . . . Well, have you asked Morton about them ?

AYLING. That did occur to me, madam.

PINKIE. Now I've hurt his feelings . . . I know I had a handkerchief . . .

(GERALD *offers her his handkerchief.*)

(*She crosses below the settee to the* R. *end.*) No, dearie, I've got one somewhere . . . (*From the mackintosh pocket she produces a ticket.*) A railway ticket. (*To* GERALD.) You can use that again.

GERALD. Must be out of date.

(PINKIE *finds her handkerchief and blows her nose.*)

PINKIE (*looking at the ticket*). No—March. You use it again, duckie—the Inspector won't tell. (*She puts the ticket on the table* R. *of the settee.*)

(GERALD *and* AYLING *both look towards the ticket. A clock strikes one.* MORTON *enters up* L.)

MORTON. Luncheon is served, sir.

(MORTON *goes out.*)

PINKIE (*moving quickly between* GERALD *and* AYLING *up to the alcove*). Thank goodness ! I'm ravenous. Are you coming along, Gerry darling ? (*She picks up the basket.*)

(GERALD *moves towards the ticket.* AYLING *steps quickly forward between* GERALD *and the table.*)

GERALD. Is that all, Inspector?

AYLING. Yes, sir, thank you. And I wouldn't dare keep Mrs. Collins from her lunch.

(PINKIE *goes out up* L. GERALD *crosses upstage to the door.*)

GERALD (*turning at the door*). Coming, Inspector ?
AYLING (*moving up a step,* R. *of the table behind the settee*). If you don't mind, sir, we'll go out this way. I just want a look round the drive.
GERALD. Yes, certainly. Do what you like.

(GERALD *goes out.* AYLING *immediately moves down to the ticket and picks it up.*)

AYLING (*looking at it and whistling*). Whew ! Liverpool to Chillington, March 28th . . . Now, what date was the National, Fred ?
GIBSON (*crossing to down* C.). Friday, March the 27th.
AYLING. Yes, but that train runs after midnight. March the 28th. And that's the man who hasn't come back from Liverpool by train for three months ! That's your straight Mr. Coates, who never went near Liverpool on the 27th ! You're a witness to where I found this ?
GIBSON. I saw Mrs. Collins find it.
AYLING. Same thing. You heard her say it was his mac., didn't you ?
GIBSON. I did.
AYLING. A ticket ! A little bit of pasteboard ! I guessed the answer the minute she produced it. You remember that train stopped outside the station ?
GIBSON. Yes.
AYLING. And a lot of passengers got off there, so their tickets weren't collected ?
GIBSON. Yes.
AYLING. Well, I think that may be about the worst bit of luck Coates ever had. (*He goes up* R. *of the table behind the settee.*) Bring those shoes.
GIBSON (*going up* L. *of the settee*). Where are we going ? (*He picks up the shoes.*)
AYLING. We'll ring up Liverpool and check up on this. Oh, and have that bag sent down right away. Come on.

AYLING *and* GIBSON *go out through the garden door. After a moment,* GERALD *opens the door up* L. *Finding the room empty, he comes in. He crosses upstage to the table* R. *of the settee and looks for the ticket.*)

PINKIE (*off*). Gerry !
GERALD. Just a minute.

(PINKIE *comes in up* L. *She stands in the doorway.*)

PINKIE. Coming, duckie ?

GERALD. Pinkie, that ticket you found—where did you put it ?

PINKIE (*coming down* L. *of the settee*). On the table, didn't I ? (*She crosses below the settee to* GERALD.)

GERALD. I thought you did.

PINKIE (*looking on the table*). Did you want it ?

GERALD. Not particularly.

PINKIE. Well, the Police must have taken it ! What a cheek ! Do you think they'll use it ?

GERALD. Yes, I think they may. (*After a little pause.*) In fact, I'm pretty sure they will.

CURTAIN.

ACT III.

SCENE.—*The same. The same day (early afternoon).*

The rain has stopped and the sun is shining through the open window. The stool L.C. has been moved slightly upstage in front of the L. end of the settee and a coffee tray now stands on it.

PINKIE *is sitting in the armchair above the fireplace. She is smoking a cigarette, and is ready to leave.* GERALD *is standing by the garden door looking out into the garden.*

For a moment after the CURTAIN *rises there is silence*

GERALD (*turning to* PINKIE). A little more coffee ?

PINKIE. No, thank you.

(GERALD *turns away again.*)

(*After a pause.*) Gerry ?

GERALD. Hullo ? (*He turns to* PINKIE *again.*)

PINKIE. Is there anything wrong ?

GERALD. Wrong ? No, nothing. Why (*He comes downstage to the* R. *end of the settee.*)

PINKIE. Well, that's the third time you've offered me more coffee, and the third time I've said no.

GERALD. Good Lord, is it really ? I'm awfully sorry. (*He sits on the settee,* R. *end.*) I'm afraid I was day-dreaming.

PINKIE. Nice dreams, I hope.

GERALD. As nice as I deserve, I expect.

PINKIE. Then they must have been nice. Gerry, there's one thing I must say before I go. It's about Donovan.

GERALD. Must you, Pinkie ?

PINKIE. I must just say this. You do believe I knew nothing about that, don't you ?

GERALD. Well of course I do.

PINKIE. Even though she is dead . . . I couldn't believe Babs could be such a fool when she had you.

GERALD. I'm not much to write home about.

PINKIE. I've got eyes in my head, dearie—not that a blind man couldn't have seen she was heading for trouble.

GERALD. It wasn't all her fault—it never is.

PINKIE. It's no use pretending—we both know it was drink. I've felt bad about it often, Gerry. When she got engaged to you I felt I ought to warn you.

GERALD. It wouldn't have made any difference.

PINKIE. I tried to keep her off it. When she was a kid I never let her into the bar, but when she grew up . . . (*She shakes her head.*) I thought she'd be all right when she married you.

GERALD. It was probably my fault she wasn't.

PINKIE. No, it'd got hold of her. You'd think after all we went

66

through with Dad . . . Funny it missed me. I like a drink as well
as the next, but I never want to take more than enough—suppose I
saw too much of it from the other side of the bar. It might have
been better if I had kept her behind the bar with me, but she was
too pretty for that in those days, wasn't she ?

GERALD. She was.

PINKIE. Oh, well, what's the good of talking ? But don't blame
yourself for anything, and don't take it too hard. (*She rises and
moves to the* L. *end of the settee and sits on the arm.*) I hope you'll
find someone else, and I hope she'll be as nice as you deserve.

GERALD (*rising*). Pinkie, please—(*he crosses to the fireplace*) don't
say that ! If you only knew how little I deserve it !

PINKIE. Well, I mean every word of it, but I won't say any more.

GERALD. No, don't. (*He turns to her.*) Have a drop more
coffee.

PINKIE. Gerry !

GERALD. Oh, sorry ! I don't know what's wrong with me.

(JOYCE *appears from off* L. *at the garden door.*)

GERALD. Oh, Joyce ! (*He goes quickly up* L. *of the settee and
crosses to the garden door.*)

JOYCE. May I come in ? (*She crosses downstage of* GERALD *to
the table behind the settee.*) I had to come back. I remembered I
never said good-bye to Pinkie this morning.

(GERALD *moves to the desk.*)

PINKIE (*sitting on the settee*, L. *end*). That's right. " Where's
Joyce ? " I said, and Gerry said you'd gone. " Gone ! " I said,
" I hardly saw her." It was those police and all their silly questions
—they put everything out of my head.

JOYCE. They've gone—haven't they ?

GERALD. Well, they didn't stay to lunch.

JOYCE. Do you think they'll come back ?

PINKIE. They're just like flies—they keep coming back.

GERALD. Pinkie's taken against the police force.

PINKIE. No, it's only that flat-footed Inspector. He and
Hoskyns can go on finding things till they're black in the face. I
still won't believe Babs came back here that night.

(MORTON *enters up* L. *He comes down to the stool* L.C.)

Are they here again !

MORTON. Who, madam ?

PINKIE. The police.

MORTON. No, madam, they are not here for the moment. (*He
moves the stool downstage to the old position.*) Your car is at the
door, madam, and I have put your luggage on.

PINKIE. Oh, thank you, Morton. (*She rises and moves to the*

chair above the fireplace.   She picks up her gloves and puts them on.)
MORTON (*to* GERALD).   Er—as Mrs. Collins has mentioned the
police . . .

(JOYCE *crosses to the open window up* R.)

GERALD.   Yes, Morton . . .
MORTON.   It's about Hoskyns' " clue", sir.
GERALD.   Yes.
MORTON.   Well, it turned out to be a pair of shoes which Hoskyns
found in my pantry, sir.   In case the police should mention the
matter to you.
GERALD.   Oh, yes, the Inspector did say something about it, but
I told them I was sure that whatever you said was right.

(PINKIE *moves to the chair down* L.)

MORTON.   Thank you, sir.   The Inspector seems to be sure that
everything I say is wrong.
PINKIE (*picking up her bag and moving to* MORTON).   Morton,
you and I must have a talk about that man sometime—I've a feeling
we'd enjoy ourselves. (*She crosses downstage to* GERALD.)   Good-
bye, Gerry. (*She gives him a hug and a kiss.*)
GERALD.   Good-bye, Pinkie.   Thank you so much for all you've
done.
PINKIE.   Nonsense, dearie.   I don't like leaving you like this,
and that's a fact.   All alone.
GERALD.   Oh, that's all right——

(MORTON *picks up the coffee tray and starts towards the door up* L.)

PINKIE (*beginning to be tearful*).   Oh, I can't bear it ! (*She goes
up* C. *above the settee.*)   Morton—will you look after him ?
MORTON.   Yes, madam, you may be sure I will do everything in
my power.
PINKIE.   Yes, I know you will.

(MORTON *exits up* L.)

(*To* GERALD.)   And if ever you feel lonely, dearie, you know where
to come . . .   No, you're not to come out with me !
GERALD (*going up to the* R. *of* PINKIE).   Yes, darling, Joyce and I
are coming to wave you good-bye.
PINKIE.   No, you're not going to see me off.   No, I mean it !
(*She crosses to* JOYCE.)   . . . Good-bye, Joyce, you will look after
him, won't you ?

(MORTON *enters up* L.   *He has* PINKIE'S *overcoat on his arm.*)

JOYCE.   Yes, I'll look after him.
PINKIE.   Oh ! (*She is crying now.*)   Oh, I'm sorry I'm being
such a fool !

(MORTON *holds the door open.*   PINKIE *crosses below* GERALD *towards
the door.*)

GERALD. Oh, shut up, Pinkie, we're going to see a lot of each other. Now come on—Joyce and I are coming out to wave to you. (*He follows her towards the door.*)

(JOYCE *crosses to up* C.)

PINKIE. No, you're not !—No, Gerry ! . . . I know just what I look like when I cry !—a big, wet cloud !

(PINKIE *exits up* L.   JOYCE *takes off her overcoat and puts it over the back of the chair* R.C.)

GERALD. You see her off, Morton.

MORTON. Very good, sir.

(MORTON *goes out.*   JOYCE *moves down* R. *of the settee.*)

GERALD. Poor Pinkie !—she's got the warmest heart in England.

JOYCE (*crossing to the stool*, L.C.). Gerry . . . Gerry, I'm sorry.

GERALD (*coming down* L. *of the settee*). Oh, my dear ! (*He meets her above the stool*, L.C.)

JOYCE. I had to come back—I had to come and say that.

GERALD. Thank God you did ! I had a feeling you might never come back.

JOYCE. I was a fool !

GERALD. You weren't. Anyone would have felt as you did.

JOYCE. It was such a shock. I couldn't think—I only saw the danger, and I wanted you to do the safest thing.

GERALD. I know.

JOYCE. You couldn't, could you ? It wouldn't have been you. Oh, Gerry, can you go on ? Can you get through ?

GERALD. I can have a damn good try. Oh, God, I thought I'd lost you !

JOYCE. Gerry ! . . .

(JOYCE *slips into* GERALD'S *arms and they kiss.*)

That was an idiotic thing to think ! Even if they find out—but they won't, will they ?

GERALD. No. (*He breaks away to the fireplace.*)

JOYCE. They've gone, haven't they ? Do you think they'll come back ?

GERALD. Oh, yes, they'll come back all right.

JOYCE. Why ? Has something happened ? Have they found out something ?

GERALD. No.

JOYCE. Have they guessed something ?

GERALD. I don't know.

JOYCE. Oh, Gerry, you must tell me !

GERALD. Well, (*he crosses below the settee to* R.C.) I'm pretty sure now that they suspect me. They think Babs came back here that night, and they think I was in Liverpool.

E*

JOYCE (*following him to the* R. *of the settee*). Oh, God ! (*Sits on the settee.*) How do they know ?

GERALD. They *don't* know. That's what I've got to cling on to all the time—they don't *know*.

JOYCE. What was that Morton said about a pair of shoes ?

GERALD (*moving up to the back of the settee*). Oh, the shoes—I must admit that frightened me to death at first. I didn't notice it till I was taking her out to the car.

JOYCE. Notice what ?

GERALD. That she had no shoes on.

JOYCE (*bewildered*). Where were they ?

GERALD. I don't know. I searched the room and the car and the drive. (*He sits on the* R. *arm of the settee.*) They simply weren't there. All the same, it was a bad moment when the police suddenly produced a pair this morning. But Morton cleared that up, thank God.

JOYCE. It wasn't the missing pair ?

GERALD. No.

JOYCE. Oh, Gerry ! . . .

GERALD. The shoes were nothing—just a bad two minutes.

JOYCE. What else ? Why do they think you were in Liverpool ? I know Buns told them, but you said that didn't matter. Or were you just comforting me ? I'd sooner know.

GERALD (*rising and moving upstage*). No, I don't think Buns by himself is worth a damn. But . . . (*He crosses up* L.)

JOYCE. But what ? Oh, Gerry, I have to drag everything out of you !

GERALD (*coming down* L. *of the settee*). Well, this morning they were quite friendly, the police. I don't think they suspected me at all. I had my story ready, and it sounded all right. Then, just as they were going, Pinkie came in, wearing my macintosh, and produced from the pocket a ticket from Liverpool. (*He comes down* L. *of the stool* L.C.)

JOYCE. A ticket ? . . . The ticket you used that night ?

GERALD (*agitatedly ; going up* L.C.). Yes, I think it must have been. She said it was dated March.

JOYCE. What happened to it ?

GERALD. The police have got it.

JOYCE. How much does it matter ?

GERALD. A good deal, I think. I told them so definitely that I hadn't come back by train for three months.

JOYCE. So now they know that was a lie.

GERALD. I'm afraid so.

JOYCE. Oh, Gerry !

GERALD (*coming down* L.C.). It serves me right—one should never boast of one's luck. All the same it was a bit hard that Pinkie—Pinkie of all people—should find that ticket in my macintosh pocket and practically hand it to the police.

JOYCE. Was that where you left it—in your macintosh pocket ?

GERALD (*going to the settee and sitting,* L. *end*). That's the maddening thing—I could have sworn I didn't. I hadn't forgotten it —I took it out of my pocket about a hundred yards this side of the level crossing and threw it away. It seemed the safest thing to do. I threw it into the bushes in somebody's garden.

JOYCE. But if you threw it away ? . . .

GERALD. Of course I couldn't have done. It was dark. It must have been some other old ticket. You see, I was telling the truth when I said I hadn't come back from Liverpool by train for three months. Except for that night, I hadn't. A ticket from Liverpool in my pocket dated March must have been that one. It must be dated March 28th.

JOYCE (*rising and crossing to the fireplace*). Then it's really serious ?

GERALD. Yes, I'm afraid it is.

JOYCE. When do you think they'll come back ?

GERALD (*rising and going to* JOYCE). Any minute now, I think. And my sweet, I don't think you ought to be here.

JOYCE (*ignoring this*). Gerry, if they arrest you ; I think you must tell them the truth.

GERALD. Yes. If they arrest me, or even if they warn me ; they haven't cautioned me, and they can't use anything I've said in evidence. If it comes to a trial—well, most of the damage is done, and I shall tell the truth. A lying statement first would only make things worse.

JOYCE. Whatever happens, I meant what I said. If you do go to prison, I'll wait for you.

(GERALD *shakes his head.*)

Oh, Gerry, don't be so damned noble and pig-headed ! It's not because I'm sorry for you ! I'm not being unselfish ! I'll wait because I can't do anything else ! Because I don't love anyone else ! Because there never will be anyone else ! Nothing will ever change me. Gerry, if things go wrong, remember that !

GERALD. I'll remember you saying it.

JOYCE. Gerry !

GERALD. It's going to be all right—I've got to get round this somehow, and I will.

JOYCE. I know you will——

GERALD. I'm going to bluff for all I'm worth up to the very last minute. And now, my sweet, you must go.

JOYCE. Gerry, I can't—I can't go home without knowing !

GERALD. You must. If things go wrong——

JOYCE. They won't ! (*She crosses downstage of* GERALD *and goes up* L. *of the settee.*)

GERALD. ——you'll hear from Philip. If it's all right, I'll ring you.

JOYCE (*turning, above the* L. *end of the settee*).   Be careful what you say.

GERALD.   Yes, I'll say . . . I'll ask you to lunch with me to-morrow.

JOYCE.   All right, I'll go.   I'll sit by the telephone.

GERALD.   Come on.   I'll see you to the gate.   (*He crosses down-stage and up to the chair* R.C.   *He picks up* JOYCE'S *coat.*)

(JOYCE *and* GERALD *move together to the garden door.*   MORTON *enters up* L.   *He closes the door behind him.*)

MORTON.   Excuse me, sir, Inspector Ayling is here, and would like to see you.

GERALD.   All right, show him in.   I'm going out for a moment but I'll be back.   (*He puts the coat round* JOYCE'S *shoulders.*)

MORTON.   Very good, sir.

(MORTON *goes out up* L.)

GERALD.   Well, the flag's down—we're off !

(JOYCE *kisses him.*)

JOYCE.   That's for luck !

GERALD.   Don't worry—I'll do it.   Come on.

(JOYCE *and* GERALD *go out through the garden door and exit* R. *past the windows.   For a few seconds the stage is empty.*   MORTON *enters up* L.   *He shows in* AYLING *and* GIBSON.)

MORTON.   Mr. Coates will be with you in a minute, Inspector.

AYLING (*turning up* C. *; brusquely*).   Where is Mr. Coates ?

(GIBSON *stands above the* L. *end of the settee.*)

MORTON.   Mr. Coates is engaged at the moment, he will be with you very shortly.

(MORTON *goes out.*)

AYLING.   I shall enjoy seeing that butler in the dock as accessory. (*He comes down* R.C.)   I hope Coates hasn't bolted.   (*He crosses to the fireplace.*)

GIBSON.   Bolted !   That's the last thing he'd do.   I tell you, Bert, if you arrest Coates on the evidence you've got, you'll make the mistake of your life.

AYLING.   I've got all the evidence I want—or I will have before I finish.

GIBSON.   Well, I can't see it your way.   (*He comes down* L. *of the settee.*)   I don't believe in the mirror, and Morton's explained the shoes.

AYLING.   Yes, I heard him.   (*Sardonically.*)   Did you believe him ?   . . . How d'you explain the ticket ?

GIBSON.   I don't, but I expect Coates will.   If he had done it, he'd have had the sense to lose that ticket.   I know Coates.

AYLING. They always make one mistake. Look here, Fred, you know as well as I do, in a case like this, you go on feeling your way, asking questions and getting nowhere, until you find someone who tells you a lie, and when you do, nine times out of ten, you've got your man.

GIBSON. That's true enough.

AYLING. I *know* he did it. The mirror, and the shoes, and the mileage, tell me he did it. The ticket *proves* it.

GIBSON. So if he can explain that ticket, he's all right ?

AYLING. Yes, the rest isn't evidence. I'll break him over that ticket. Coates told me he hadn't returned from Liverpool by train for three months, so when I found that ticket, I had him just like that.

GIBSON. All right—have it your own way. Don't forget the blessed Judge's rules. Are you going to caution him ?

AYLING. Not just yet, I'll give him a chance first to explain the ticket. But if he can't, I'll ask him to come down to the station and make a proper statement.

GIBSON. All right, Bert—don't say I didn't warn you.

AYLING. I'm going to try a bit of bluff first of all. See if he won't save us trouble.

GIBSON. Bluff ! You'll find he can keep his end up at that game.

AYLING. Maybe—maybe not. He's got a pretty big stake up.

(GERALD *passes the windows from off* R.)

GIBSON. I doubt if that'll put him off. He . . .

(AYLING *warns* GIBSON *with a gesture.* GERALD *enters by the garden door. He comes to the* R. *end of the table behind the settee.*)

GERALD. Sorry to keep you waiting.

AYLING. That's quite all right, sir. It's too bad to worry you again, but I didn't quite finish this morning.

(GERALD *crosses to the desk and picks up his pipe and tobacco jar.*)

GERALD. You've got some more questions, have you ? (*He crosses down* C. *below the* R. *end of the settee.*)

AYLING (*advancing above the stool* L.C.). Yes, I have. But I'm afraid they're much the same questions that I asked you this morning.

GERALD. Well, that's all right as long as you don't mind the same answers.

AYLING. You see, we're still working on the theory that Mrs. Coates came back here that night.

(GIBSON *crosses upstage to the garden door.*)

GERALD (*filling his pipe*). Still, are you ? Have you any evidence to support that theory ?

AYLING. I told you some of it this morning, sir.

GERALD. Did you ?

AYLING. I mentioned that Mrs. Coates' mirror and shoes were found here on the Saturday morning.

GERALD. Oh, Hoskyns' story—yes, of course. (*He puts the tobacco jar on the table* R. *of the settee.*) I'm afraid I didn't take that very seriously. No, I thought you might have something definite. (*He sits on the settee,* R. *end.*)

AYLING. The mirror's more definite than it was, sir. We know for certain now that it belongs to the bag Mrs. Coates had with her. There's also the speedometer of Mrs. Coates' car.

GERALD. Oh yes, I don't think I've heard about that.

AYLING. No, there are one or two things you haven't heard yet, sir. Just before Mrs. Coates went to Liverpool, she took her car down to Renton's Garage here to have it serviced. In fact, Mr. Donovan fetched it from there on the Thursday morning.

GERALD. Yes, I believe he did.

AYLING. The garage slipped a Tecalemit card in the pigeon-hole of the dash. It shows the exact mileage when the car was serviced.

GERALD. Oh, yes, it would. Renton's always do that.

AYLING. Well, the total mileage since serviceing, until the car was found with the body in Liverpool was—give me the figures, Sergeant.

(GIBSON *crosses upstage to the* L. *end of the settee. He holds out his notebook to* AYLING *and points to the entry.* AYLING *takes a step upstage to him. He continues to watch* GERALD.)

GIBSON (*pointing*). Seventy-nine point seven, sir.

AYLING. That's right, seventy-nine point seven.

(GIBSON *drops back up* L.)

Now, we also got from Mr. Donovan the exact route he took that car, and we drove the car over that same route again. That came to fifty-five point two miles. (*He looks at* GERALD *and adds slowly :*) Which leaves a difference, unaccounted for, of twenty-four point five miles . . . Does that suggest anything to you, sir ?

GERALD. No, I'm afraid not.

AYLING. We also drove the car from the Adelphi to the front door here, and then back to the spot in Selborne Road where the car was found. That came to twenty-four point two miles . . . Now do you see what I'm driving at, sir ?

GERALD. I'm awfully sorry to be dense, I'm afraid I don't.

(AYLING *moves to the arm-chair above the fireplace and sits.*)

AYLING. Well, the mileage unaccounted for was twenty-four point five, and Liverpool to here and back was twenty-four point two. There isn't very much difference, is there ?

GERALD. Oh, I see. I'm sorry I got muddled with the figures. You mean that's a suggestion that the car came back here that day and then back to Liverpool ?

AYLING. Exactly, sir. A pretty strong suggestion, too.

GERALD. That was very clever of you.

AYLING. You hadn't thought of that, sir ?

GERALD. Oh, no, no—that's most ingenious. (*He rises and crosses to the fireplace.*) Of course, all it actually proves is that the car was driven some twenty-four odd miles that you can't account for. And that's always assuming that Mr. Donovan gave you an accurate account of his journeyings.

(AYLING *rises and comes down to the stool* L.C. GIBSON *crosses upstage to the garden door.*)

AYLING. Well, of course it *might* be just a coincidence, sir, but we don't think so. We think it's just one more pretty clear hint that the car did come here.

GERALD (*looking for matches on the mantelpiece*). Did anybody see it on the way ?

AYLING. No one that we've found yet.

GERALD (*taking a spill from the mantelpiece.*) Of course, it was very foggy that night. (*He bends down to light the spill in the fire.*)

AYLING. Was it difficult (*he strikes a match*) driving, sir ?

(GERALD *drops the spill. He straightens up, turns to* AYLING *and takes the match.*)

GERALD. Oh, I think it must have been—don't you ? (*He lights his pipe.*)

AYLING. I suppose it was the fog that made Mr. Darling think he saw you coming back on the twelve forty that night ?

GERALD. Partly. Also he'd been what he calls splitting bottles. I don't think he splits them fine enough.

AYLING. He can't have been very drunk, sir. He got home safely.

GERALD. Oh, instinct, Inspector, and he's had a good deal of practice, too. (*He crosses downstage to the* R. *end of the settee.*)

AYLING. There's another question, sir—one I haven't asked you yet. (*He moves to the fire and turns to* GERALD.)

GERALD (*turning to* AYLING). Go on. (*He moves slightly towards the* L. *end of the settee.*)

(*There is a pause.* AYLING *and* GERALD *face each other.*)

AYLING. Did you see your wife that night ?

GERALD. Inspector, I thought I'd made myself perfectly clear. I told you I spent the evening here alone—I've told you that several times. Do you really expect me to say, at this stage—" Oh, I forgot to tell you—my wife dropped in after dinner " ? (*He sits on the settee,* L. *end.*)

AYLING. No, sir, I don't . . . (*He pauses.*) I wonder if I might be quite frank ? (*He sits on the* R. *arm of the arm-chair above the fire.*)

GERALD. I think it would save a lot of time and trouble if you were.

AYLING. Well, sir, this is *not* a case of murder. The doctor's evidence is that your wife's injuries were not very serious. Now, it seems to me quite possible—in fact, very likely—that someone had a bit of a row with your wife that night.

GERALD. I think that's fairly obvious.

AYLING. But whoever it was, he had no intention of killing her. I fancy it must have been a very nasty shock to him when he found she was dead.

GERALD. Oh, I think it must have been, don't you ?

AYLING *(confidingly)*. Now, that's where I think he lost his head, sir. If he'd sent for the police, or a doctor, then, there wouldn't have been all this trouble.

GERALD. No, but, as you say, he must have thought he'd murdered her. That was bound to mean trouble.

AYLING. Yes, but you'd be surprised how little people know about the law. I expect this man, whoever he is, probably still thinks it's a hanging matter if he comes forward.

GERALD. Oh, surely not ! For one thing, he'll have read the account of the inquest—sure to have.

AYLING. Oh, yes, sure to . . . he might even have attended the inquest. *(He pauses.)* Well then, let's say he knows it isn't a hanging matter. Even so, he probably doesn't realise that if he comes forward frankly now and explains what happened, he'll only receive a very light sentence—something absolutely nominal.

GERALD. Would he really ? I shouldn't have thought so. It's still manslaughter. He probably doesn't want to go to prison at all.

(GIBSON *grins.*)

AYLING *(airily)*. Well, he might be found guilty of manslaughter, sir, though I doubt even that. But of course, if he's trying to get away with it, he's certainly making things worse for himself—that's what he ought to remember. Because we'll find him out in the end, that you can be sure of.

GERALD. I naturally hope you do.

AYLING *(after a pause)*. Well, sir ?

GERALD. Well ?

(There is a pause.)

AYLING. Have you any . . . *(he pauses)* suggestions ?

GERALD. Oh, I'm sorry ! I didn't know you wanted advice.

(GIBSON *grins broadly.*)

Yes, I think there's probably a great deal in what you say. I believe it might be worth your while to get something like that put in the papers. After all, if you're absolutely stuck, and haven't a shred of evidence against the chap you might bluff him into giving himself up. It's worth trying, anyway. (*He rises.*) It might come off. (*He crosses to the desk.*)

AYLING. You think we have no evidence, sir ?

GERALD. Well, you were just going to tell me when we branched off. (*He knocks out his pipe in the ashtray on the desk.*)

AYLING (*crossing below the settee to* R.C.). This ticket is interesting. (*He produces the ticket.*)

GERALD. W'nich ticket ?

(GERALD *turns and meets* AYLING *at* R.C. GIBSON *moves to the* R. *end of the table behind the settee and watches anxiously.*)

AYLING. The one Mrs. Collins found in your mackintosh pocket, sir. You didn't notice I'd taken it ?

GERALD. Yes, I did, as a matter of fact.

AYLING. Can you explain how it came to be in your pocket ? It's dated March the 28th.

GERALD. March 28th ! This year ?

AYLING. This year.

GERALD. *Do* they put the year on tickets ?

AYLING. They do.

GERALD. How very careful of them. I never noticed that . . . No, I can't tell you how it got into my pocket.

AYLING. It is strange, sir, because you told me this morning you hadn't returned from Liverpool by train for at least three months.

GERALD. I don't think I have.

AYLING. And yet . . . March 28th—the day after the National. Were you in Liverpool at all that day, sir ?

GERALD. Yes, I went to my office in the morning and came down again before lunch, but I went both ways by car.

AYLING. And you weren't up there earlier, sir ? Very early, in fact—just after midnight ?

GERALD. I've told you I wasn't.

AYLING. Because that's when this ticket was issued, soon after midnight. Just about in time for the twelve forty-two. You still say you didn't buy it, sir ?

GERALD. I do.

AYLING. And yet it was the twelve forty-two that Mr. Darling thought he saw you on.

GERALD. I thought he said on the platform in Liverpool.

AYLING. Not much difference. You still say he was mistaken ?

GERALD. I do. (*He breaks away and crosses below the settee to the stool* L.C.)

AYLING (*turning*). You do, sir ? Then just let me put the facts quite plainly.

(GERALD *turns.*)

Mrs. Coates left the Adelphi at ten fifteen. Her car, in which her body was subsequently found, had been driven the exact distance from the Adelphi to this house and back to Selborne Road. A mirror which was missing from Mrs. Coates' bag was found in this room next morning. A witness has said he saw you returning from Liverpool on the train that left there at twelve forty-two——

GERALD. That witness——

AYLING. One moment, sir. Many passengers who travelled on the twelve forty-two failed to give up their tickets, and a ticket— *this* ticket—issued just before the twelve forty-two left Liverpool, is found in your mackintosh pocket. *Now* do you see, sir, why the ticket is significant ?

GERALD. Oh, yes, I do.

AYLING. Then, sir, once more, have you any explanation of how it came to be in your pocket ?

GERALD. None. I'm sorry, Inspector, (*turns away to the fire*) I can't tell you anything more about that ticket.

AYLING. No, sir ? Would you care to make a statement ?

GERALD (*turning*). Good God ! What have I been doing for the last half hour ?

AYLING. Just talking, sir. I mean, would you care to come down to the station now and make a statement which can be taken down and typed, so that you can sign it ?

GERALD. About that ticket ? (*He comes above the stool* L.C.)

AYLING. No, Mr. Coates—about all your movements on that night.

GERALD. Are you arresting me ?

AYLING. Not yet, sir. I propose to caution you and then take a statement.

GERALD. Then I can refuse to come ?

AYLING. You can, Mr. Coates, but I don't think you'd be wise to. (*He pauses.*) You see, you'd have to come in the end.

(GERALD *hesitates for a moment, reluctantly making his decision.*)

GERALD. Oh, very well, I'll come. I'd like to get hold of my solicitor if I may. Is that allowed ?

AYLING. Certainly, sir. You're entitled to be legally represented.

GERALD. All right, I'll ring him. (*He crosses downstage to the desk, sits in the chair and takes up the telephone.*)

(AYLING *crosses downstage to the fireplace.* GERALD *dials* " 0." AYLING *and* GIBSON *watch him.* BUNS DARLING *appears from off* R. *at the garden door. He has a mackintosh slung over his shoulder.*)

BUNS (*entering*). Hullo, Gerry—— (*He sees the two* POLICEMEN.) Oh, sorry—you busy ?

GERALD. Yes.

BUNS (*coming to the back of the chair* R.C.). Oh, sorry ! Good afternoon, Inspector. (*To* GERALD.) I won't keep you, old man. I only want . . .

GERALD (*viciously*). Whatever it is you want to say, will you go round to the front door and ring the bell ?

BUNS (*flustered*). Yes, of course—good Lord, yes, of course I will. Sorry I butted in—I only wanted to return your mac. I'll give it to Morton.

(BUNS *goes out through the garden door and off* L.)

GERALD (*into the 'phone*). Hello, exchange? I want . . . (*Suddenly he swings round to* AYLING *and covers the mouthpiece with his hand.*) My God !—did you hear that ?
AYLING. What, sir ?
GIBSON. I did, sir.
GERALD (*to* GIBSON). Get him back !
GIBSON (*running out through the garden door ; calling*). Mr. Darling ! Mr. Darling, sir !

(GIBSON *goes out and off* L.)

GERALD (*into the 'phone*). Hello—Exchange—sorry, my mistake. (*As he puts down the receiver.*) My mistake !
AYLING. We hardly want Mr. Darling in here just now, sir.
GERALD. You may not, Inspector, but I do.

(BUNS *enters by the garden door. He is followed by* GIBSON.)

Now, Buns, what did you say just now ?

(GIBSON *crosses upstage to the* L. *end of the settee.*)

BUNS (*coming to the back of the chair*, R.C.). I said I was terribly sorry for butting in, old man. I didn't see the Inspector at first.
GERALD. No, after that ?

(BUNS *looks blank.*)

Just as you went out.
BUNS. I said I only wanted to return this. (*He hangs the mackintosh over the back of the chair.*)
GERALD. My mackintosh ?
BUNS. Yes.
GERALD. How long have you had that ?
BUNS. Must have taken it last time I dined here. I haven't been here since.
GERALD (*to* AYLING). Your witness, Inspector.
AYLING (*to* BUNS.) When was it you dined here, sir ?
BUNS. Well, when was it, Gerry ? A Saturday, wasn't it ?— Yes, that's right. Saturday after the National. I must have grabbed your mac. when I was going home.
AYLING. And you've had it ever since, sir ?
BUNS. Yes, I'm afraid I have. (*To* GERALD.) Sorry, and all that, Gerry. Quite a mistake, of course—I only noticed it this morning. It's exactly like mine, you know, only it's a bit older— lets the rain in over the shoulders.

GERALD. Oh, what a shame. (*He crosses above the settee to the door up* L.) I'm *so* sorry you've been inconvenienced. I'll get yours.

(GERALD *goes out up* L.)

BUNS (*moving to the* R. *end of the table behind the settee*). Good Lord, Inspector, what's the joke ?
AYLING. There's no joke, sir. (*He crosses downstage and up* R.C. *to* R. *of the chair* R.C. *He examines the mackintosh.*)
BUNS. Well, I mean, what's all the fuss about ? Not going to arrest me, are you ? (*He laughs.*) I mean, mine's a better mac. than his.

(AYLING *replaces the mackintosh on the chair.* GERALD *comes in up* L. *with the other mackintosh.*)

GERALD (*at the door*). Is this it ? (*He throws the mackintosh to* BUNS.)
BUNS (*catching it*). Yes, that's it.

(GERALD *closes the door.*)

AYLING. Can you identify it for certain, sir ?
BUNS (*indignantly*). Identify it ? Good Lord, I know it's mine !
AYLING. Is it marked ?
BUNS. Oh ! . . . I expect so. (*He crosses to the window up* R. *and searches in the neck of the mackintosh.*) I always tell my man to mark everything—find I'm a bit apt to leave things about. Yes, here we are—A. J. D. (*He shows the marking to* AYLING.)
AYLING. In that case, sir, a ticket which was found in one of the pockets would be yours ?
BUNS (*cautiously*). What sort of a ticket ?
AYLING (*producing the ticket*). A railway ticket—this one, sir, from Liverpool to Chillington, dated March 28th.

(GERALD *comes down* L. *of the settee.*)

BUNS. Yes, well, that was mine. I came home by train that night. You know, I told you about that, Inspector—I came down by train and the train stopped outside the station, so I never gave up my ticket. Why ? Nothing wrong in that, is there ?
AYLING. Nothing, sir. Here's your ticket. (*He hands it to* BUNS.)
BUNS (*taking it*). I don't want this. Good Lord, Inspector, I hope you don't think I'd use that again ?
AYLING. I don't care whether you use it or not, sir.
BUNS. Oh ! (*Nevertheless, he puts the ticket in his waistcoat pocket. He crosses to the table* R. *of the settee.*) Look here, Gerry, if my ticket's been bothering you, I really am most awfully sorry.

(AYLING *comes down* R. *by the desk.*)

GERALD. No, it's the Inspector you ought to apologise to.

BUNS. Why ? Did he think it was a clue, or something ?

GERALD. I think he hoped it might be.

BUNS. What, my ticket ? (*He turns to* AYLING.) Oh, but I've got an alibi ! Yes, yes, I know what you're going to say. (*He makes hastily for the garden door.*) So long, Gerry.

(BUNS *goes out through the garden door and off* L. *with his mackintosh.*)

GERALD (*coming down* C.). Well, Inspector ?

AYLING. Well, sir—that's that. We shan't have to trouble you now.

GERALD. Are you sure ? No trouble.

AYLING. I'm afraid we owe you an apology, sir, but I hope you see that until that ticket was explained we had to take the line we did.

GERALD. I saw that all along.

AYLING. Thank you, sir. (*He crosses up* C. *to* GIBSON.) Well, sir, now that's cleared up, I'll be getting back to Liverpool.

GERALD (*crossing to the desk*). Shall we be seeing you down here again ?

AYLING. It depends on how things go, sir. I don't think there's much more to do at this end now. Good afternoon.

GERALD. What about you, Gibson ? We'll be seeing you about the place, I suppose ?

GIBSON. Oh, yes, sir, they don't think enough of me to move me to Liverpool. The Inspector was saying this morning, sir, guarding chicken runs is about my mark. He thinks I'm a bit slow for . . .

AYLING (*interrupting*). Come along, Gibson. (*He goes to the door up* L.)

GIBSON. Good afternoon, sir.

(AYLING *goes out up* L.)

GERALD. Good-bye, Gibson.

(GIBSON *follows* AYLING *out up* L. GERRY *sits at the desk. He puts the telephone on his knee and faces downstage.* MORTON *enters up* L. *He carries the shoes in a parcel.*)

Have they gone, Morton ?

MORTON. Yes, sir.

GERALD. What have you got there ?

MORTON (*moving above the settee*). That pair of shoes, sir. The Inspector gave them to me as he was leaving. He said he had finished with them.

GERALD. I think they're satisfied now. I don't think they'll come back.

MORTON. I hope not, sir. I hope you will be given a chance to forget it all. (*He crosses to the chair at* R.C.)

GERALD. Thank you, Morton.

(MORTON *takes the mackintosh off the chair and crosses upstage towards the door up* L.)

MORTON (*turning up* L.C.).   Tea at half-past four, sir ?

GERALD.   No, no tea.   I'm going out.

MORTON.   Very good, sir.   (*He continues to the door.*)

(MORTON *goes out up* L. *with the mackintosh.*   GERALD *dials a number.*)

GERALD (*immediately he has finished dialling*).   Have you been sitting by the 'phone all the time ?   . . . Well, I wanted to know if you'd lunch with me to-morrow ?

QUICK CURTAIN.

FURNITURE AND PROPERTY PLOT.

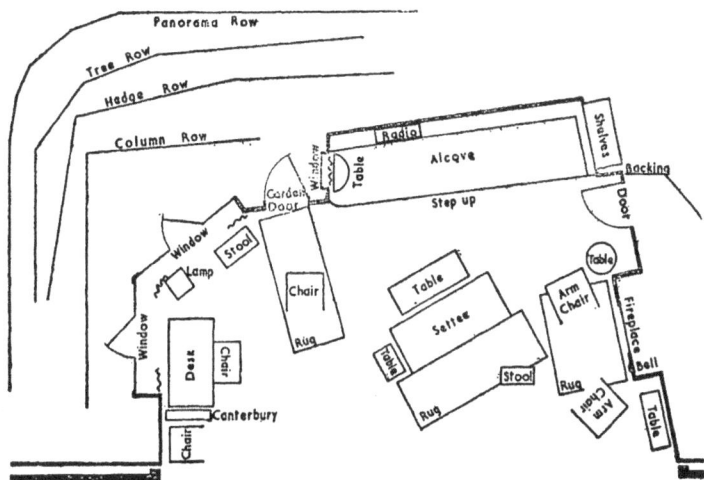

Throughout the play :

On Stage.—2 Easy chairs.

    2 Upright arm-chairs.

    Settee. *On it :* 3 Cushions.

    Desk. *On it :* Ashtray, Bowl of Pipes, Pencil, Inkwell, Blotter, Paper-weight, Paper-knife, Matches, Cigarette box, 8 Cigarettes, Telephone, Telephone message pad, Desk lamp.

    1 Upright chair.

    2 Stools.

    Stand for table lamp. *On its lower shelf :* 3 Books.

    Gate-legged table. *On it :* Ashtray.

    Long table. *On it :* Ashtray, Bowl of pot-pourri, Matches, Cigarette box, 7 Cigarettes.

    Drink Cabinet or table.

    Canterbury. *In it :* Magazines.

    Round pedestal table. *On it :* Table lamp, Ashtray, Globe, Vase of Jasmine.

    Wall table. *On it :* 2 China ornaments, Vase of flowers.

    On Mantelpiece : 2 Candlesticks, 2 China figures, Clock, Ashtray, Matches, Box of spills.

    Above Mantelpiece : Portrait, 2 Wall brackets.

    In Fireplace : Fender, Bellows, Dogs, Poker, Tongs, Shovel, Hearth-brush.

On Alcove Shelf : 8 China ornaments, Radio, 2 Book-ends,
10 Books, Table lamp, Lacquered wooden
box, 2 odd Books.

In Alcove Cupboard : 8 Silver Cups and Trophies.

Below Alcove Shelf : Prop. Books.

On Window-ledge : 5 Plants, Ornamental bottle.

5 Rugs.

3 Heavy Curtains.

6 Sporting prints.

1 Picture of a horse.

3 Other pictures.

PROLOGUE

On Stage.—On Desk : Liverpool Evening Paper.
Magazine.

In Top R. *Drawer of Desk :* Torch.

On Stool up R. : Magazine.

On Gate-legged Table : Bowl of crocuses.

On Long Table : Book with uncut pages.
Tumbler.

On Drink Table : Small tray.
Bottle of whisky.
Soda syphon.

In Fireplace : Small log.

On Alcove Shelf : Tobacco jar.

Off Stage R.—Suitcase (GERALD).
Framed piece of glass (for window tapping).

Personal.—BABS : Handbag, Powder compact, Lipstick.

Garden door closed.

Curtains drawn.

At end of Scene strike.—BAB'S coat and bag.
Suitcase.
Tumbler.
Tray and Whisky bottle.

ACT I.

SCENE 1.

On Stage.—On Drink Table : Tray with 5 Tumblers, 2 Sherry Glasses,
2 Cocktail Glasses, Decanter of Whisky,
Bottle of Gin, Decanter of Sherry, Soda
Syphon, Lemonade Jug.

Off Stage L.—Clock strike.
Door bell.

Personal.—PHILIP : Notebook and Pencil, 2 £1 notes, Matches.
    GERALD : Handful of silver coins.
    BUNS : 1 £1 note, 2 10s. notes.
    JOYCE : Handbag.

Garden door closed.

Curtains drawn.

At end of Scene strike : Magazine from settee.
                     Magazine from armchair down L.
                     Evening paper from chair R.C.

Move : 2 Glasses from mantelpiece to drink table.
       1 Glass from table above fire to drink table.

SCENE 2.

On Stage.—*Below Chair* R.C. : Card table.
    R. *of Card table :* Chair from down R.
    L. *of Card Table :* Chair from desk.
    Below Card table : Stool from up R.
    On L. *arm of Settee :* Copy of " The Times."
        On Card table.—*Upstage* (GERALD) : Marker, 7 tricks taken, 5 Cards to play.
                     Downstage (JOYCE) : Marker, 5 cards to play face up.
                     R. (BUNS) : Marker, 1 Trick taken, 5 Cards to play.
                     L. (PHILIP) : Marker, 5 Cards to play.
                     Between PHILIP *and* JOYCE : Ashtray, 2nd Pack.
    On Desk : JOYCE'S bag.

Off Stage L.—Clock strike.
    Door bell.
    Knocker.

Garden door closed.

Curtains drawn.

At end of Act strike.—Card table.
    Tray and Drinks.
    All Glasses.
    " The Times."
    Bowl of Crocuses.

ACT II.

On Stage.—*Replace* : Chair at Desk, Chair below Desk, Stool up R.

> *On Gate-legged Table* : Bowl of anemones.
>
> *On Desk* : PINKIE's Handbag.
>
> *On Mantelpiece* : Pipe.

Off Stage L.—Basket and Secateurs
Bunch of Daffodils
Mackintosh with Ticket and Handkerchief in R. pocket ⎫(PINKIE)
Mirror in cellophane cover (AYLING).
Pair of shoes, wrapped (GIBSON).
Clock strike.

Personal.—GERALD : Cigarette case.

> GIBSON : Notebook and pencil.
>
> JOYCE : Handbag.

Garden door open.

Upstage Window open.

Downstage Window closed.

Curtains open.

At end of Act strike.—Box of matches from Mantelpiece.

> *Move* : Stool L.C. below L. end of settee.
>
> GERALD's pipe to desk beside tobacco jar.
>
> Cushion from back of chair above fire to seat.

Replace : PHILIP's book on alcove shelf.

ACT III.

On Stage.—*On Stool* L.C. : Tray with Coffee pot, Milk jug, Sugar basin, cup and saucer.

> *On Table above fire* : Coffee cup and saucer.
> *On Chair above fire* : PINKIE's gloves.
> *On Chair below fire* : PINKIE's bag.

Off Stage R.—Mackintosh (BUNS).

Off Stage L.—PINKIE's overcoat
Shoes, wrapped ⎬(MORTON)
Mackintosh (GERALD).

Personal.—AYLING : Box of matches, Ticket
GIBSON : Notebook.

LIGHTING PLOT.

Property fittings required :—
2 Wall brackets (*controlled together*).
3 Table Stands (*separately controlled*).
1 Desk Light.
Fire.

THE MAIN ACTING AREA is between the settee and the fireplace.

BATTENS or FLOODS should be used for the general lighting from above.

FOOTLIGHTS or F.O.H. SPOTS should be used to counteract shadows on the face.

Spots, on No. 1 Bar immediately behind the proscenium, should, if possible, be used for lighting the acting area. They must cover the areas presumed to be lit by the Wall Brackets and standard lamps. (*Possible colours are* 3 *Straw ;* 4 *Amber ; Open White.*)

SMALL FLOODS or STRIPS (3 *Straw*) will be required to light the Hall backing. A small Spot (5 *Orange and* 10 *Middle Rose mixed*) will be required for the firelight.
    All Floods and Spots should have dimmers in circuit. If Borders are used instead of a ceiling it may be found necessary to use extra lighting equipment behind them to avoid shadows on the top of the set.

PROLOGUE. Night.

Wall brackets, Desk lamp, Table lamp by fireplace ON, covered by Spots.

Fire and Fire-spot ON.

Battens (or Floods) and Footlights (19 Blue) ON.
No light outside windows.

At Cue.—BLACK-OUT.

ACT I. SCENE 1.—Night.

The same except : *add* Table lamps by window and in alcove ON, and
                    Spots to cover.
                    Desk lamp OFF.
                    Battens (or Floods) and Footlights (54 *Pink*) ON.

No cues.

SCENE 2.—The same.

At Cue.—Table lamp by window OFF, and Spots covering.

ACT II.

Daylight.

The apparent source of light is from the windows.

A FLOOD or FLOODS will be required to light the Garden Backing.

87

A PAGEANT LAMP or SPOT (3 *Straw*), which should be more powerful than any used on the stage, should be directed through the window down R. towards the alcove up L. to simulate sunlight.
Fire and Fire-spot ON.
All fittings OFF.

Cue 1.   GERALD :   " . . . you'd never have seen me again."
Slow fade of sunlight and light on Garden Backing.   (2 minutes.)

Cue 2.   PINKIE *enters by the garden door.   She carries basket of daffodils.*
Slow fade IN of sunlight and light on garden backing.   (2 minutes.)

ACT   III.

The same as ACT II but sunlight may be changed to 54 *Pink* to give added warmth and the angle of it should be shifted slightly downstage.

The colours indicated are intended only as a guide.   The actual colours employed must depend on the colour scheme of the set and furnishings. They should be so chosen that differentiation can be made between daylight and artificial light and it will probably be found of advantage to colour the Spots for artificial light and the Battens or Floods for daylight.

www.ingramcontent.com/pod-product-compliance
Lightning Source LLC
LaVergne TN
LVHW051754080426
835511LV00018B/3318